DETAILING LIGHT

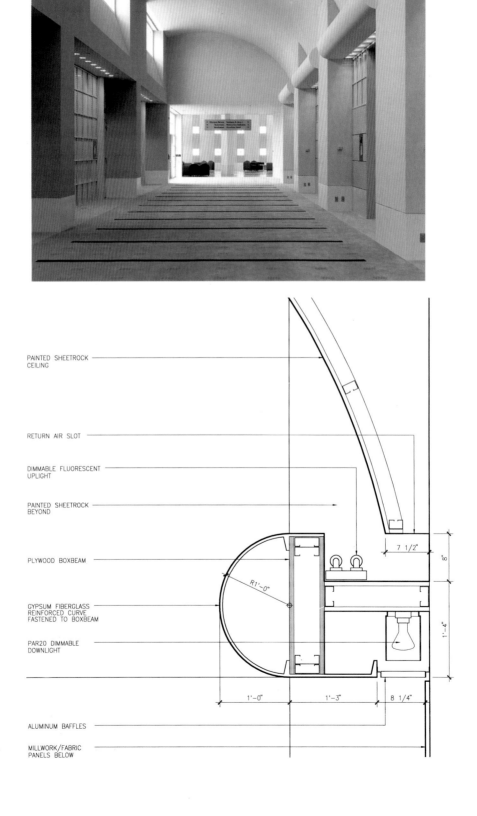

PAINTED SHEETROCK
CEILING

RETURN AIR SLOT

DIMMABLE FLUORESCENT
UPLIGHT

PAINTED SHEETROCK
BEYOND

PLYWOOD BOXBEAM

GYPSUM FIBERGLASS
REINFORCED CURVE
FASTENED TO BOXBEAM

PAR20 DIMMABLE
DOWNLIGHT

ALUMINUM BAFFLES

MILLWORK/FABRIC
PANELS BELOW

7 1/2"

8"

R1'-0"

1'-4"

1'-0"

1'-3"

8 1/4"

DETAILING LIGHT

INTEGRATED
LIGHTING
SOLUTIONS
FOR RESIDENTIAL
AND CONTRACT
DESIGN

JEAN GORMAN

WHITNEY LIBRARY OF DESIGN
an imprint of Watson-Guptill Publications, New York

Senior Editor: Roberto de Alba
Associate Editor: Micaela Porta
Designer: Bob Fillie, Graphiti Graphics
Production Manager: Ellen Greene

First published in the United States in 1995 by Whitney Library
of Design, an imprint of Watson-Guptill Publications, a division
of BPI Communications, Inc., 1515 Broadway, New York, NY 10036.

Library of Congress Cataloging-in-Publication Data
Library of Congress Cataloging-in-Publication Data
Gorman, Jean, 1958-
Detailing light: integrated lighting solutions for residential and
contract design / Jean Gorman
    p. cm.
Includes index.
ISBN 0-8230-1341-3
1. Lighting, Architectural and decorative. I. Title.
NK2115.5.L5G67 1995
729'.28—dc20   95-10915
                                     CIP

**729.
28
GOR**

Photographs appearing on pages 55, 123, and 125 used
by permission from The Walt Disney Company.

Distributed in the United Kingdom by Phaidon Press, Ltd.,
140 Kensington Church Street, London W8 48N, England.

Distributed in Europe (except the United Kingdom, South and
Central America, the Caribbean, the Far East, the Southeast, and Central Asia)
by Rotovision S.A., Route Suisse 9, CH-1295 Mies, Switzerland.

Manufactured in Italy
First printing, 1995

2 3 4 5 6 7 8 9 / 02 01 00 99 98

CONTENTS

FOREWORD

When Elsie de Wolfe surprised New York society in 1898 by redecorating her Irving Place apartment in white and gold, she not only established a legitimacy for the interior design profession but made an intrinsic connection between an emerging technology and the design of architectural space. The shock of the new in this case was simply a movement away from the heavily paneled dark rooms of the late Victorian period to a lighter, brighter, cleaner world illuminated with electric light. Gone were the gaslight sconces, chandeliers, and soot-producing candles: A new era had arrived.

Light sources and lighting techniques have today developed beyond the mere application of new technology into a rich and complex world where the manipulation of artificial light has evolved into a profession of its own. This evolution, driven by technological advances, has enhanced our most useful sense of vision such that we can now create, as demonstrated by the examples to follow, surprising, emotive interiors where the relationship between architecture and the detailing of light make the same intrinsic connections as did Mme. de Wolfe.

As often occurs in a world of choice, the bad parallels the good, and designers are regularly guilty of solely seeing lighting design as the specifying of lighting fixtures. The missed opportunities of this approach fail to connect with the emotional values light has as a component of architecture, one that can support our vision and perception of space as truly memorable.

Think about lighting this way: Imagine yourself in total darkness, imagine the kind of light that would suit your mood, describe to yourself—either through previous experience or invention—the type of light that would best suit and focus that mood. The more profound experiences are often the moments when a simple but dynamic connection is made between light and architecture, a shaft of sunlight streaming through a window and highlighting interior furnishings; the softness of a wash of light on a textured wall; the romance of candle light at the dinner table; the drama of a stage follow spot on a performer; the mystery and hope of light at the end of a tunnel.

These examples exist, the technology to support them exists, and the design solutions are now made easier. This simplified process is the foundation of today's architectural lighting profession: an architect's vision married to the technological sophistication of the lighting designer striving to produce seamless projects that are triumphs of space, texture, and color. This idealized world is rarely attained, education in this realm is still in its infancy, the value of it to clients is not emphasized by architects and designers, the cost is divisive, the poetry is often lost. The challenges currently are to find ways to allow the poetry of lighting design to exist, to educate, and to integrate an ever-increasing specialization pressured by varying agendas which are conceptually divorced from architectural exploration.

As you review and find inspiration from the examples that follow, see them within the larger context of the struggle architects and lighting designers undertake in exploring solutions. See them as contributions to the broader understanding of lighting design. And see them finally as a way of seeing.

PAUL HAIGH, AIA
April 1995

INTRODUCTION

While lighting technology has certainly come a long way since Thomas Alva Edison invented the light bulb in 1878, its artful integration into contemporary architectural settings is frequently given less attention than it rightfully deserves. The collection of details I have gathered and presented in this book represents to my mind some of the most beautiful examples of the sophisticated use of light within a wide array of contexts built over the past five years.

Since its evolution over the course of the last century, lighting design at its best has become a sophisticated art form. One of its early and most talented practitioners, the late architect and lighting designer Richard Kelly, defined the basic elements of good lighting design as ambient illumination, focal glow, and sparkle. Assuming that most well-designed spaces take these fundamentals into account, rather than reviewing overall lighting concepts, compositions, or schemes, I have focused instead on details that illustrate ways in which these elements have been refined in relation to their architectural context, enhancing that architecture's beauty beyond merely illuminating its forms. In addition to fulfilling technical concerns such as appropriate illumina-tion levels or accurate color rendition, the details in this book emphasize the use of light as an extension of the architecture which reinforces the artistic integrity of the architect's or the design-er's vision.

Many of the lighting details featured represent common lighting techniques, yet the illustrated variations on these standard themes reveal the subtleties involved in artfully interpreting an appropriate response to a unique con-text. Chosen for their aesthetic appeal more than for their technical considera-tions, they range from the simplest of standard fixtures manipulated to extend the language of the architecture to sophisticated, elaborately constructed custom fixtures to integrated architec-tural solutions. What they all have in common is their beauty and intrinsic connection to the overall intentions of the design. Their effectiveness as light-ing solutions can best be judged by qualified lighting designers.

Working within the constraints of the modest budgets of most projects completed within the last five years, architects and lighting designers alike have been forced to become more imag-inative in doing their work. While the drawings range in quality from relatively rough sketches to construction docu-ments to refined presentation drawings specifically created for the book, they all reveal the various levels of thought that have gone into the development of the specific details presented.

I am indebted to the architects and lighting designers who were willing to share their ideas in this book, especially those who prepared new drawings to illustrate their designs. Equally impor-tant are all of the photographers with-out whose contributions this book would not have been possible. I am grateful as well to my editor, Roberto de Alba, for his insight and support, to Micaela Porta for her expert editorial work and assistance in tending to the many details involved in pulling the pieces of the book together, and to my family, friends, and colleagues—particu-larly to *Interiors* magazine's publishing director, Dennis Cahill, and its editor-in-chief, M.J. Madigan—for their patience and encouragement in the writ-ing process.

As an interested observer of architec-ture and interior design, it is my hope that the work of the talented architects, interior designers, and lighting designers featured on the following pages will inspire many others to more fully exploit the artistic potential of light.

JEAN GORMAN
New York City
May 1995

PUBLIC SPACE

CONTINENTAL AIRLINES, LA GUARDIA AIRPORT

Location: Flushing, New York

Architect: Smith-Miller+Hawkinson Architects

Lighting Designer: H.M. Brandston and Partners

Structural Engineer: Ove Arup & Partners

Manufacturers: Composite Engineering (Kevlar panels); Trypyramid Structures (stainless-steel rods, fittings); KSK (steel truss); Pilkington (glass); Lettera Graphics (signage); Linear Lighting (uplights, downlights).

Date Completed: November 1992

Photography: Eric Cobb (fixture); Laurie Hawkinson (truss system)

Smith-Miller+Hawkinson created an image for Continental Airlines that not only sets it apart from the rest but also offers the practical benefit of appropriate task lighting. The new terminal in La Guardia Airport, designed by William Bodouva & Associates, was under construction when the architects undertook the project, so two prevailing conditions were critical in determining the architect's highly site-specific response: One was that the terminal was a glass building oriented south; the other was a space plan in which the location and orientation of the ticket counters in relation to the rise and fall of the sun had already been established. In devising a physical element to define the airline's identity within this context, the architects created a structure evocative of the streamlined qualities of aircraft design by constructing it with aviation materials and technology.

Three key lighting issues were addressed: keeping the sun out of the ticket agents' eyes, keeping direct light off the computer screen, and providing task light where necessary. The lighting designers determined that far too much natural light entered the building. Therefore, the architects designed an extensive nine-bay, 270-foot-long suspended truss system in which the key element is an extremely thin cantilevered canopy that acts as a sunshade against the bright light.

The canopy is composed of 36, 7-foot-wide-by-14½-foot-long custom-fabricated panels of a lightweight, 3/4-inch-thick material known as Kevlar, one of three primary materials that play a role in completing the truss system.

The other two essential materials in this system are steel and glass, which form the components that support both the system itself and the architects' aesthetic aim of creating a lightweight structural system that contrasts with, conditions, and improves the existing space. The primary materials are so artfully combined and mutually dependent that the system appears and functions as a single fixture modulating the light. However, each material was also selected for its specificity to the particular function it serves in the truss system as a whole.

Kevlar's unique composition, for instance, allows the material to be both lightweight and extremely strong—attributes the architects deemed necessary in responding to their design's application as the canopy. It is composed of a honeycomb core sandwiched between carbon-fiber sheets and coated with epoxy resin. The entire composition was "layed up" in a mold and baked, creating an ultimate tensile strength 20 times greater than that of fiberglass. The material's ability to be molded also makes it ideal in this application in that the panels' leading and rear edges could be shaped to reach the specific points needed to block the incoming natural light.

Supporting the cantilevered panels of the canopy at each bay are a series of 12-foot-long steel armatures, hung from columns along the lobby's north wall at

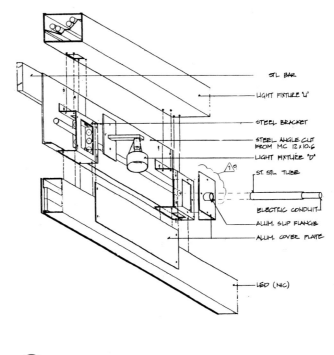

STL BAR
LIGHT FIXTURE 'U'
STEEL BRACKET
STEEL ANGLE CUT FROM MC 12 x 10.6
LIGHT FIXTURE 'D'
ST. STL TUBE
ELECTRIC CONDUIT
ALUM. SLIP FLANGE
ALUM. COVER PLATE
LED (NIC)

③ EXPLODED AXONOMETRIC
— NOT TO SCALE

Continental Airlines

a height of 8 feet 7 inches from the floor. Each steel armature is composed of an assembly of steel plates, a carbon steel bar, and stainless-steel pipes through which electrical conduit and a data cable are threaded. Assisting the steel armature in its support of the Kevlar panels at each bay are six stainless-steel rods that extend upward to a small steel bracket bolted to the column 23½ feet above the ground. Two stainless-steel rods are actually fastened to a glass triangle, the final component that completes the truss system.

The system's nine, 67-inch-by-67-inch-by-54-inch isosceles triangles are composed of two sheets of 3/8-inch-

thick laminated tempered glass. In typical architectural applications, glass is secured on a minimum of two sides and exposed only to the bending forces of wind loads. But the glass elements in this system are ingeniously employed as structural elements by securing one of the triangle's corners to the steel armature, another to the stainless-steel rods that extend upward to the bracket on the north wall, and the third to the Kevlar panels. By leaving all three sides of the triangle free and securing only its corners, some axial and compressive stresses caused by dead and live loads are transferred through the glass and back to the column.

In order to achieve the seamless unity of each of the primary components in the system, the nature of each material and how they would be joined was carefully considered. To keep the glass from experiencing torsion and cracking, for example, the holes at each connection point were detailed with custom stainless-steel fittings, using naval fabrication technology, and stainless-steel pins passing through the holes are buffered with spherical bushings to prevent transferring any moment forces to the glass. To resist punching and compression of the Kevlar panels and to help distribute the load, the connections in the canopy were reinforced with aluminum blocks

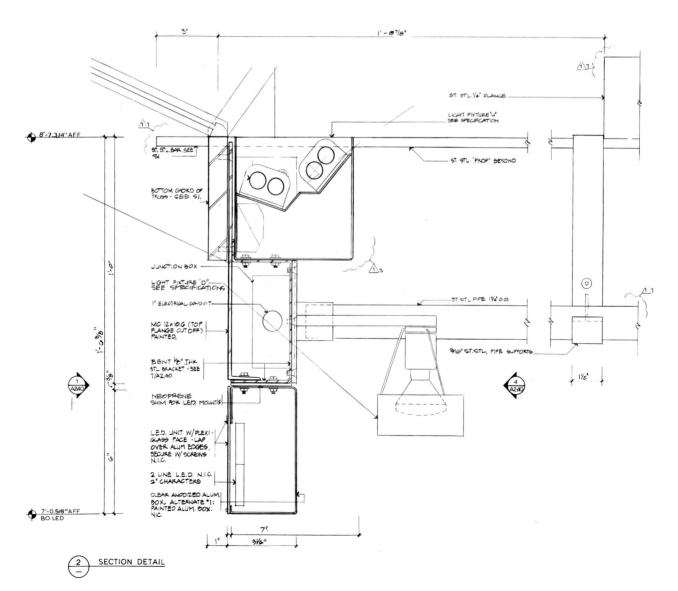

2 SECTION DETAIL

and carbon-reinforced sheets. The entire assembly is designed to act as a single truss capable of supporting its own weight, the load of a person walking on the top surface in case of an emergency, and the loads of the light fixtures and LED equipment mounted at their ends beneath the Kevlar panels.

The light fixtures mounted to the steel truss beneath the canopy are also attached to nine, 30-foot-long-by-6-inch-high-by-1-inch-deep steel bars, linked end to end with fittings across the 270-foot length of the structure. A steel angle bolted to each bar supports the three lighting components that comprise the fixture: An uplight containing 39-watt biaxial high-lumen compact fluorescents; an incandescent 50-watt PAR 20 narrow flood down-light; and an LED display fixture. Power is supplied to the fixtures at each bay by the electrical conduit threaded from the

wall through the steel pipe, which connects directly to a custom stainless-steel bracket that covers a junction box. The junction box, with knock-outs on all sides, allows a variety of fixtures to be wired from a single point. The down-light, which provides task light on the desk below, is mounted to another stainless-steel bracket bolted to the steel angle. The fluorescent uplight fixture, which reflects off the canopy above and provides ambient light, rests on and is bolted to the tops of the two brackets. And the LED unit, which provides display lighting information, is mounted to the bottoms of the brackets. The electrical conduit is concealed from view by an aluminum plate.

At the juncture where the lighting elements are mounted, the lighting, structure, and program are fully integrated. At the point of interaction between the agent and customer, the

uplights evenly illuminate and enhance the profile of the canopy, the most provocative element of the structure, which is painted gray-white to provide ambient bounce light. The two rows of uplights were switched separately for two levels of operation: a high level of indirect light during the day (to compensate for the high level of daylight flooding the space) and a lower level in the evening. The lamp's cooler color temperature of 3,500 degrees Kelvin complements the incoming daylight and metal halide sources within the main terminal. The custom-designed direct downlights—regularly spaced and baffled to keep direct light out of the agents' eyes—provide a broad band of incandescent light on the counter and offer recommended illumination levels and good color rendition for reading and writing. The structure is now occupied by US Air.

CORNING CORPORATE HEADQUARTERS

Location: New York, New York

Interior Designer: Donovan and Green

Lighting Concept: Donovan and Green

Lighting Designer: Jerry Kugler Associates

Manufacturers: CSL (halogen MR-11 fixtures); Edmund Scientific (dichroic filters, mirrors, and prisms); Maltbie, Inc. (steel laminate surface and exhibit fabrication).

Date Completed: June 1992

Photography: Wolfgang Hoyt

The Corning company, while perhaps best known for its glass cookware, has produced an array of products ranging from decorative vases to laboratory glass to railroad signal lights. At this point in the company's evolution, a major part of its business is liquid crystal display, fiberoptic, and laser technology. When its international headquarters in the Steuben building in New York were designed, Corning asked designers Donovan and Green to create an identity for its entry that would reflect the company's current high-tech agenda. In doing so, the designers chose to celebrate Corning's long-standing involvement with both glass and light by creating a compelling graphic display of colored light.

In developing the presentation, the physics of light was explored by manipulating it with dichroic filters, mirrors, and prisms. Working with lighting designers Jerry Kugler Associates, the designers used the 50-foot-long walls of the narrow entry hallway as canvasses upon which animated flashes of colored light were projected. Concealed behind fascias at the tops of the walls, 50 double-contact, bayonet-based, very narrow MR-11 halogen spots are fitted with condenser lenses and adjustable irises. This allows their beams of light to be precisely focused to under 2 inches in diameter.

The lamps were not only chosen for their ability to be narrowly focused, but also for their white light, which could be separated into all of the colors of the visible light spectrum. Positioned 1 foot on center, the lamps' slender beams of light are aimed through various dichroic

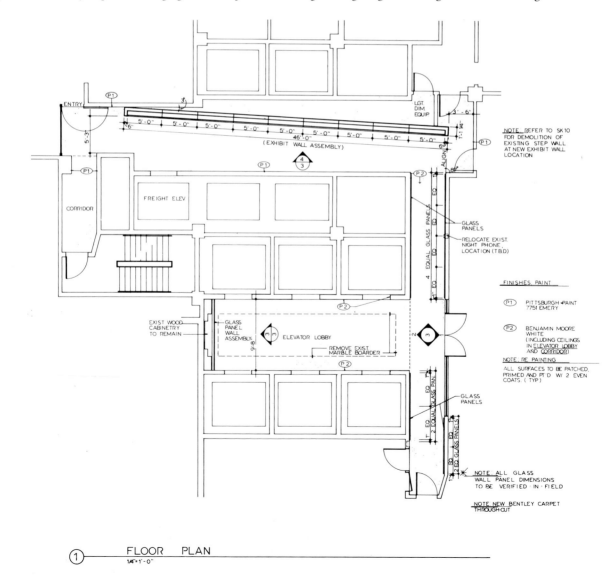

① FLOOR PLAN
1/4" = 1'-0"

Corning Incorporated
Steuben Offices

filters, which are mounted at the center of the wall and alter the color of the light. The angles of the filters also play a role in creating the desired effects. Subtle shifts in color are generated by allowing the light to pass through the filters either perpendicularly or obliquely. After passing through the filters, the light is then aimed and projected through a series of randomly placed prisms and mirrors which refract and reflect each beam to create multi-hued, feathery sprays of light on the surface of the walls.

Each wall is composed of a steel laser table surface, which is bisected with a 6-inch-wide horizontal band of stock aluminum. The laser table surfaces are highly specular to reflect the beams of light as much as possible and create the elongated flashes. They are also covered with a slightly textured lacquer to catch the light and create the softer, feathered effect. Mounted to tapped holes in the aluminum bands, the filters, prisms, and

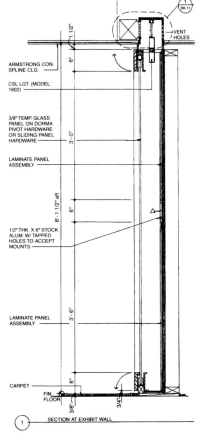

mirrors, custom-designed by Donovan and Green, create the illusion that the light emanates from the central band. A sort of abstract expressionist painting of light is created by the random arrangement of filters, mirrors, and prisms, which allow the light that passes through them to scatter in all directions. Each wall of colored lights is covered with floor-to-ceiling panels of 3/8-inch-thick tempered glass, which are mounted on pivot or sliding hardware in the fascias for access to the lamps.

To animate the display, the light sources are connected to a computer that creates an ever-changing choreographed dance of colored light over the course of the day. Every fifth light is connected to a dimming channel, which is programmed to fade the sources in a timed sequence, thereby producing a variety of kinetic patterns. Low-voltage PAR 36 downlights illuminate the center of the corridor without interfering with the effects of the light display.

13

ONE PEACHTREE CENTER

Location: Atlanta, Georgia

Architect: John Portman & Associates

Lighting Designer: H.M. Brandston and Partners

Manufacturers: Light rolls: N.L. Corporation (PAR 56 lamps; A21/T3 Traffic signal lamps; steel frame; glass rods; louvers). Domed ceiling cove: National Cathode (cold cathode lamps); Custom Plastics (Plexiglas panels; aluminum ribs).

Date Completed: July 1992

Photography: Timothy Hursley

Detail One: Light Rolls

An evolution of architect John Portman's well-known hotel atria designed in the '70s and '80s appears in appropriately subtler form in his lobby interior for One Peachtree Center, a downtown Atlanta office building. Though more subdued than his hotel atria, One Peachtree's lobby is still a far cry from traditional office lobbies in that the architect continues to explore a key design philosophy, "the explosion of space." The sophisticated, sometimes whimsical, forms of the sculpted lobby—including Portman-designed works of art—are enhanced by lighting features that were developed through intense collaboration between the architect and the lighting designers H.M. Brandston and Partners. Two special lighting features in the lobby stand out as significant and integral features of the design: a series of integrated granite-capped light roll fixtures and a dramatic domed ceiling cove in the very center of the elevator core.

While much of the general illumination in the atrium comes from the sun during the day, the lighting designers used incandescent spots to light the many works of art in the lobby and fluorescent uplights concealed in the catwalks to brighten the ceiling. The light roll fixtures above the stone bench rolls at the perimeter of the lobby reveal Portman's classic touch of decorative accent light and sparkle. But instead of leaving the bulbs exposed, as was typically done in his earlier buildings, the lamps in the light rolls are cleverly diffused, creating a subtler sparkle more appropriate for this space.

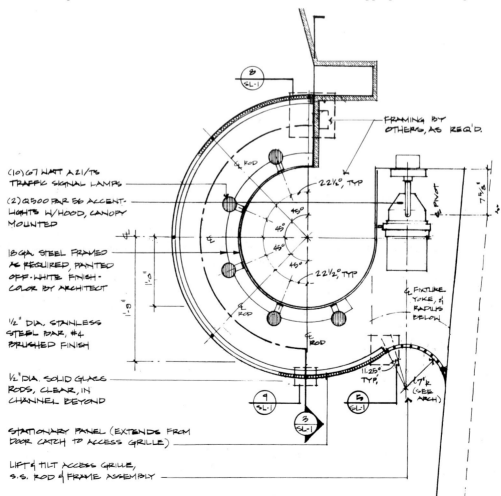

(10) 67 WATT A21/T3 TRAFFIC SIGNAL LAMPS

(2) Q500 PAR 56 ACCENT LIGHTS W/HOOD, CANOPY MOUNTED

18 GA. STEEL FRAMED AS REQUIRED, PAINTED OFF-WHITE FINISH - COLOR BY ARCHITECT

1/2" DIA. STAINLESS STEEL BAR, #4 BRUSHED FINISH

1/2" DIA. SOLID GLASS RODS, CLEAR, IN CHANNEL BEYOND

STATIONARY PANEL (EXTENDS FROM DOOR CATCH TO ACCESS GRILLE)

LIFT & TILT ACCESS GRILLE, S.S. ROD & FRAME ASSEMBLY

FRAMING BY OTHERS, AS REQ'D.

22 1/2°, TYP.

45°

22 1/2°, TYP.

CL FIXTURE YOKE, & RADIUS BELOW

11.25° TYP.

Located in the negative void between two granite-clad columns, each light roll fixture appears to be an extension of the bench below it. The light roll's rounded form echoes that of the bench, and is perched at a carefully calculated 28 feet above the lower lobby floor and a comfortable 8 feet above the main lobby bridge. The fixtures punctuate the perimeter of the atrium with sparkle, illuminate the granite roll bench below, and urge the eye upward toward the canted plaster brackets that visually appear to support the ceiling.

The ten 67-watt A21/T3 traffic signal lamps contained within the light rolls are mounted on either side of a wireway wrapped around an almost cylindrical interior steel frame. A diffusing shade—composed of dozens of 2-foot-long solid clear glass rods (each 1/2 an inch in diameter) placed side by side and fixed into place between two stainless-steel channels with a silicone sealant—wraps around the perimeter of the sconce and shields the fixtures from direct view. While the shade modifies Portman's tradition of exposed lamps, it upholds the intended dynamic sparkling effect by serving as a prism that fractures the light and creates the image of kinetic filament. Composed as a single unit, the fixture is slipped into place between two granite-clad forms capping its sides, and is detailed at the top with a piano-hinged door secured to the structure, allowing the entire shade to be lifted for access.

To provide additional light on the slanted granite below the light roll, a 500-watt PAR 56 directional spot light hidden behind the fixture washes the wall and illuminates the niches between the columns. The fixture is hooded and canopy-mounted above a louvered grill that partially blocks its direct light. The grill lifts and tilts out for access to the lamp. All of the lamps in this fixture were chosen to complement the rubbed and sanded light gray stone and warm light accenting the art, and to contrast with the daylight and cool fluorescents. The traffic signal lamps were also selected for their extended life, which averages 8,000 hours. In this setting their life is extended even further by dimming; even though they remain on 24 hours a day, they are relamped only once every three years.

One Peachtree Center

Detail Two: Dome

The luminous domed ceiling cove, which crowns the center of the lobby, signals the termination of the stepped arches of the elevator core on the main floor at One Peachtree Center. Originally intended as a simple vaulted dome, it evolved into a decorative umbrellalike cone after architect John Portman found a stonecutter's blade on the site during construction and decided to recreate it as an enlarged design motif.

The architects designed a canopy, constructed of black-painted aluminum and light green Plexiglas, to fit within the dome, while lighting designers H.M. Brandston and Partners specified two rows of cold cathode lamps to fit in a cavity around its perimeter and illuminate the dome. The lighting designers selected the cold cathode sources to match the cooler fluorescents in the building's atrium and to contrast with the warmer incandescents used in the elevator colonnade. Because the cold cathode lamp is bendable, it also provides even illumination around the entire perimeter of the cove.

The canopy's intricate construction prompts three different effects from the single source of cold cathode light. The first is rear illumination from the light emanating from the cove and bouncing off the white vaulted ceiling through the light green plastic, which was sandblasted on one side to diffuse the light. The second is the bounced light seen directly through the gaps between the metal ribs supporting the curved planes of Plexiglas. Finally, there are glimmers of sparkle created where the light grazes the canopy directly. The architect intended to create additional sparkle by adding a series of circular mirrors, which were to be mounted to the top side of the canopy on small rods, creating twinkles of reflected light (see drawing). Budget constraints, however, prevented this detail from being realized.

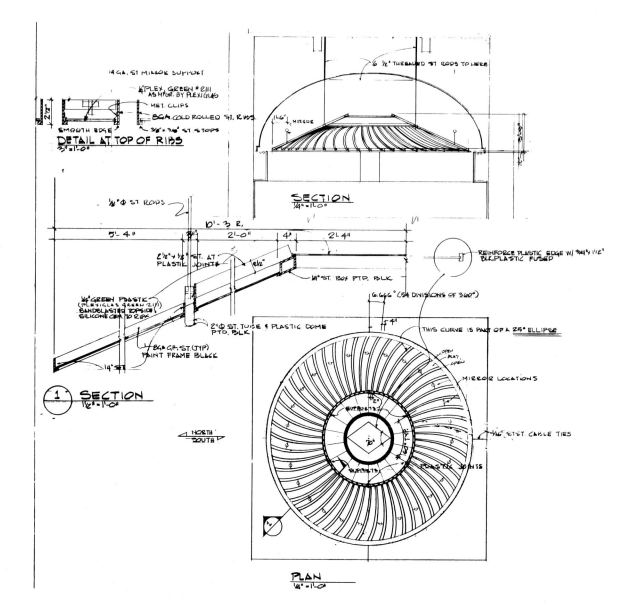

SCOTT MEDNICK ASSOCIATES

Location: Culver City, California

Architect: Eric Owen Moss, Architect

Lighting Designer: Eric Owen Moss

Lighting Consultant: Saul Goldin and Associates

Manufacturers: Philips (fluorescent lamps); Slimline by Sentinel Lighting (fixture).

Date Completed: May 1990

Photography: Todd Conversano

In his adaptive re-use of a group of existing warehouse buildings in Culver City, architect Eric Owen Moss explored "alternative" building techniques which resulted in a series of elaborate details that emphasize the notion of "technology." For example, in offices the architect designed for Scott Mednick Associates, a video graphics and advertising firm, a central corridor defined by a hierarchical system of ribs, ducts, and conduits analogously express the rational limits of technology with many of the very components that epitomize it. At the junctures where wooden box conduits containing power and data cables meet existing columns, for example, the cables are allowed to extend uninterrupted along the length of the corridor through arched metal casings which protrude from one conduit, wrap around the column, and penetrate another conduit on the column's other side. An extension of the visual vocabulary that is part of the technological narrative informing the project is a series of custom light fixtures in front of the offices along the development's main public corridor.

Positioned adjacent to the glazing system facing the SMA offices, the light fixtures were created as design elements to signal the offices and supplement the general illumination in the public corridor. Rising four feet from the floor, they were designed to punctuate the terminus points of the walls within the office which divide one space from another.

Each fixture is composed of two 40-watt T-12 fluorescent fixtures mounted to two steel angles. The angles are bolted to the wall stud and shielded by two bent perforated steel scrims, which protect the lamp, diffuse its light, and are affixed to the steel angles by zinc-plated J-shaped threaded rods. In turn, these rods hold the perforated screen in place while contributing to the visual language by echoing the form of the arched metal casings. They also act as a protective bar to prevent inadvertent contact with the lights. In order to limit the size of the fixtures, remote ballasts were concealed in the wall directly behind the light.

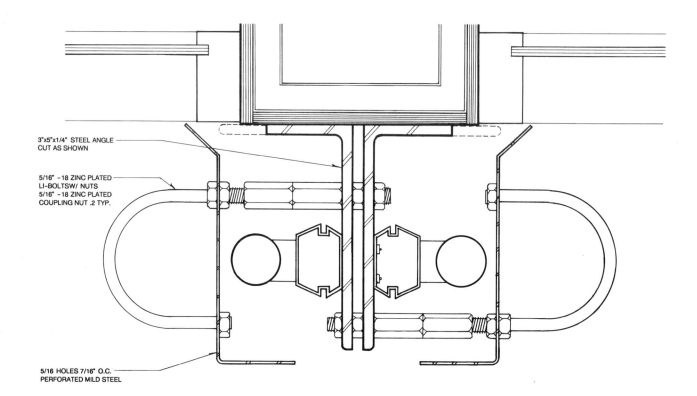

3"x5"x1/4" STEEL ANGLE
CUT AS SHOWN

5/16" -18 ZINC PLATED
LI-BOLTSW/ NUTS
5/16" -18 ZINC PLATED
COUPLING NUT .2 TYP.

5/16 HOLES 7/16" O.C.
PERFORATED MILD STEEL

VERTICAL LIGHTS @ END WALLS
3/4" = 1"

Southern Science Center, National Biological Service

Location: Lafayette, Louisiana

Architect: Guidry Beazley Ostteen Architects and Eskew Filson Architects

Lighting Designer: Cline, Bettridge, Bernstein Lighting Design, Inc.

Manufacturers: GE (PAR lamps); L.S.I. (track fixture); GE (triphosphor fluorescents); NuArt (fluorescent fixture); GE (A lamps).

Date Completed: February 1992

Photography: Sharon Risedorph Photography

The Southern Science Center is the new wetlands research laboratory of the U.S. Biological Service. Located on the grounds of the University of Southwestern Louisiana, it houses administrative offices and labs where research is conducted on wetlands loss, contaminants, and wintering water fowl. Designed by Guidry Beazley Ostteen Architects with Eskew Filson Architects, the 62,600-square-foot facility is organized around a large central spine that serves as a general meeting area for scientists while also dividing the structure's public and private spaces. While the scale of the spine is grand, its interior is defined with basic materials—drywall, a metal ceiling, and wood floors—graciously composed to create a bright inviting space for informal meetings. Simultaneously accentuating its lofty, 29-foot-high vaulted ceiling and lending it a humane sense of scale, a series of custom-designed monumental wall sconces, designed in conjunction with Cline Bettridge Bernstein Lighting Design, elegantly and appropriately reinforce the modular and material rhythm of the architecture.

The 10-foot-tall sconces were designed to punctuate the bays on one side of the spine and complement the light streaming in from clerestory windows on the other. Positioned above pilaster columns articulating the length of the spine, the sconces are composed of T-shaped steel frames supporting

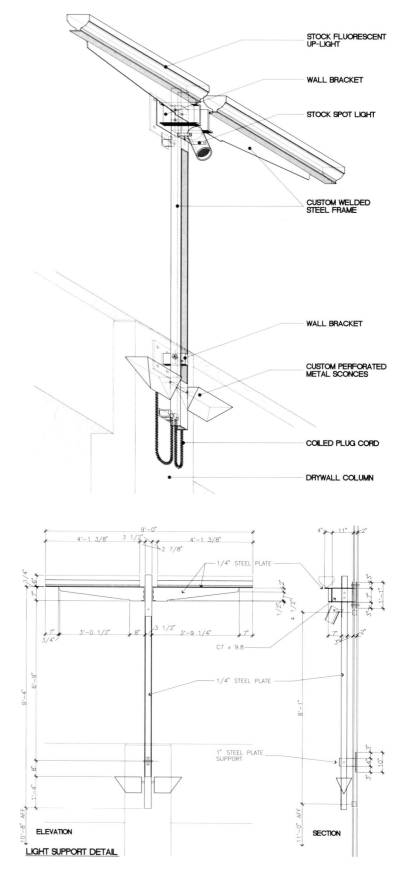

STOCK FLUORESCENT UP-LIGHT

WALL BRACKET

STOCK SPOT LIGHT

CUSTOM WELDED STEEL FRAME

WALL BRACKET

CUSTOM PERFORATED METAL SCONCES

COILED PLUG CORD

DRYWALL COLUMN

9'-0"
4'-1 3/8"   3 1/2"   4'-1 3/8"
2 7/8"
4"   11"   2"

1/4" STEEL PLATE

1/4"
6"
7"

7"   3'-0 1/2"   8"   3 1/2"   3'-9 1/4"   7"
3/4"

C7 x 9.8

1/4" STEEL PLATE

1" STEEL PLATE SUPPORT

ELEVATION

LIGHT SUPPORT DETAIL

SECTION

three different light sources, each fulfilling a distinct function. Flanking the frame's central post, two heavy-duty industrial type fixtures with wide-spread reflectors containing two 4-foot-long triphosphor fluorescents each cast diffuse light on the white-metal ceiling, which reflects 10 footcandles of ambient light toward the floor. Mounted just beneath the fluorescents, a 250-watt PAR 38 lamp in a modified standard track fixture is aimed at a 15-degree angle to accent the interior materials and punch a pool of light on the wood floor. At the very base of the frame, two long-life, 135-watt A lamps, contained within custom perforated white aluminum housings, cast diffused uplight along the walls and warm light on people's faces, bringing the scale to a human level. Each of the sources can be switched separately, and all provide infill light and reduce contrast caused by the sunlight during the day.

An intrinsic part of the design, each sconce was devised as an artfully assembled kit of parts. The straightforward, functional use of materials in the space is reflected in the sconces with each piece, including the curly cords powering the sources at the base of the frame, being clearly visible. Painted in the same icy blue as the steel trusswork supporting the ceiling, the sconces are also cost-effective and energy efficient; when government officials conducted the value engineering study, they determined that the lighting elements could not be improved upon.

THE STAR COURT AT DARLING PARK

Location: Sydney, Australia

Architect: Lend Lease Design Group and Eric R. Kuhne & Associates

Interior Designer: Eric R. Kuhne & Associates

Lighting Designer: Steven Bliss of T. Kondos Associates

Manufacturers: Indirect ceiling floods: RLM Lighting (PAR 38 spots); Dimtronix (computer system); Devon Glass (filters). Ceiling oculus: Alias Sign Co. (neon). Celestial fiber optics: Optic Light Cables (fiber optics, lamps, motor-driven assembly). Global clock: Philips (fluorescents); Architectural Graphics (custom manufacture of glass plate, stainless-steel cutouts, metal casing, Tasmanian Blackwood bezel assembly). Pitchi lamps: Cydonia Glass Works (glass castings); Louis Polsen (electrical components and assembly). Niche lighting: Reggiani (dichroic halogens); Alias Sign Co. (neon); RLM Lighting (PAR 38 flood).

Date Completed: October 1993

Photography: Michael Chittenden

Detail One: Ceiling

Perhaps the most significant space in Darling Park, a harborside development in Sydney, Australia, is its principal interior gateway and public space called the Star Court, a carefully orchestrated composition of integrated art forms, indigenous materials, and regional imagery expressing Australian culture. A bas-relief frieze depicting the history of Australian commerce surrounds the perimeter of the triangular prism-shaped volume, which is capped by a 3-pointed semi-spherical dome illustrated with iconic imagery of Australian lore. Enchanting details, including lattice-work and floors of native Rose Gum and Brushbox woods, echo the Australian outback. Light plays a significant role in this space, most strikingly as a theatrical accompaniment to the drama portrayed in the room, but more subtly it enhances the architecture's inherent sculptural qualities.

Several integrated lighting components reflect off the architecture in the room to create luminous surfaces, while as few point sources as possible offer direct light for intensely focused or decorative effects. The idea was to create a ceremonial atmosphere that would lift the Star Court from the rest of the commercial space. Because it is in the shadow of a 28-story tower, the designers relied heavily on artificial light to create its character.

The ceiling is where the most concentrated attention to lighting is paid. The lighting required to illuminate its

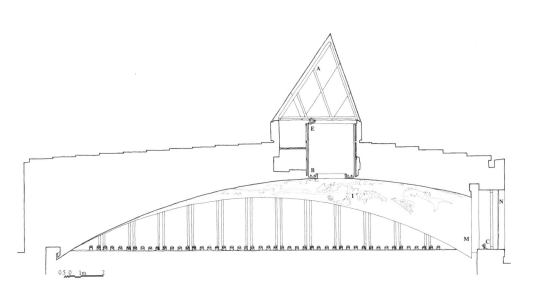

A Crystal Lantern Etched Glass Skylight 15mm White Neon 60mA

B Oculus Double Tube Curved Neon Cove Lighting 12mm Neon

C Ceiling Wash Spotlights With Colorfilters Par 38 E 27 RLM

D Recessed 'Spill' Light 50mm 6x 8,3 20/50W

E Adjustable Par 56 Spot RLM

F Recessed Diocroic Downlight (Sunlight Mojo)

G Recessed Floorwashers ERCO-Par 56 NSP

H Adjustable Par 56 Spot

I 723 Fiber Optics 'Stars'

J Concord 'Tangent' Recessed Beam Flood Fitted With 200W, 300W, 500W Linear Tungsten Halogen Lamps

K Storefront 240V Par 50 Quartz 300W NSP Recessed Spot

L Daylight Crescent Garden Window Wall With Trellis

M Handkerchief Vault Celestial Dome Ceiling

N Eyelid Clerestory Daylight

O Wood Lattice Screen Filter

P World Clock With Philips Standard 36W/29 Flourescent Tubes

Q Skylight

R 'Pitchi 'Lamp Fixture

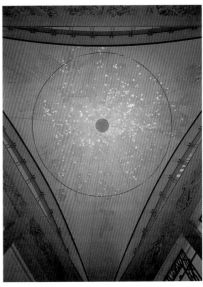

unique surface can be divided into roughly three parts: a series of computer-controlled flood lamps hidden along the base of clerestory windows beneath the dome that reflect off the dome's surface; a neon cove surrounding the ceiling's central oculus and a crystal skylight above it; and a plethora of fiber-optic points creating an elaborate celestial starscape of the constellations of the southern hemisphere.

The hidden flood lamps were used to fully illuminate the dome and set a mood according to the event occurring in the space. In order to evenly and completely illuminate the ceiling surface, 37 100-watt PAR 38 spot lamps were positioned one foot eight inches on center on each of the three sides of the volume. The lamps are mounted to a continual track on fully adjustable PAR lamp gimble rings, and are individually aimed to throw light as far as possible for even distribution and to avoid hot spots. A pelmut edge shields the lamps from view from below. Finished with perforated aluminum acoustical tiles and painted a matte putty-gray, the ceiling surface is 78 percent reflective. When grazed by the 111 lamps, it becomes a luminous source of reflected light. The efficiency of the tungsten halogen lamps was required to fully illuminate the ceiling surface and provide the proper lumen output level to sufficiently light the space below.

Computer-controlled with custom software and covered with amber-, cyan-, and magenta-colored glass filters, the flood lamps simulate the full spectral characteristics of diurnal and nocturnal daylight throughout the four seasons of the year. The system was designed to simulate natural atmospheric conditions, which are eradicated in any downtown area because of the ambient light from buildings. Equipped with six different sequences, the software program allows the flood lamps to recreate any time of day or night, under sunny or cloudy skies, at different times throughout the year, and to automatically change over the course of six hours.

The oculus in the domed ceiling in the Star Court at Darling Park serves as an ethereal focal point. Its 7½-foot-high interior walls are painted a deep iridescent violet in contrast to the muted tone of the ceiling. The base of the oculus contains a cove of cool white, 15 millimeter, 60 milliamp neon, so that the oculus itself appears to float. Above the oculus is an etched glass tetrahedral skylight. It functions as a helioscope, allowing a disk of sunlight to move across the floor through the course of the day. Another neon tube around the top of the oculus illuminates the skylight at night, creating the appearance of a glowing crystal atop the structure from the exterior. And one adjustable 300-watt PAR 56 narrow spot surface-mounted at the top of the oculus illuminates the ceremonial butterfly stair.

The night sky is depicted on the surface of the dome surrounding the oculus, with images of Aboriginal and Australian myths illustrating the constellations and glistening stars that accurately mimic the firmament of the southern

Star Court

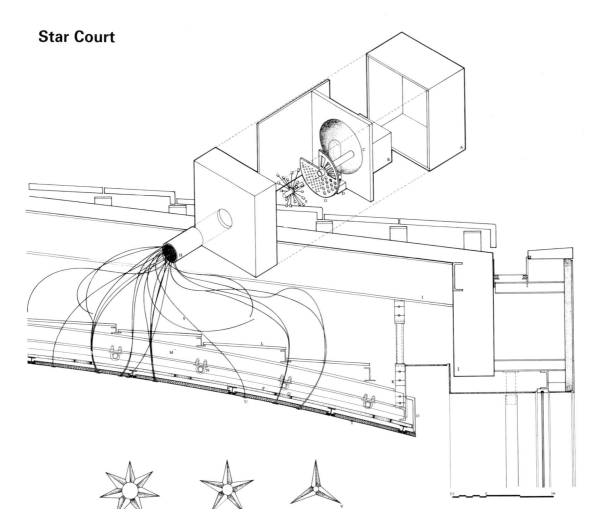

A   Stainless Steel Metal Housing
H24.5cm x W21.5cm x L45.5cm

B   240 Volt 50 Hertz Motor Box

C   Reflective Coated Surface

D   150W Metal Halide 3000° K Bulb

E   Diffuser

F   'Satellite Paddles' To Provide Light
Flow Interruption To The Fibers

G   Motor Driven Mechanical Vane
Paddle To Set The Intensity Level Of
Light To The Fiber Optic Bundles

H   Fiber Optics Bundle

I   Structural I-Beam

J   Concrete Structure

K   Purlin

L   Removable Aluminum Floor Access
Panels On Aluminum Sections Fixed
To U-Beams

M   Structural I-Beams Positioned
Radially From The Oculus

N   Structural Steel Support Framing

O   13mm Plasterboard

P   Cast-On-Site Fiberglass Reinforced
Plaster Dome

Q   150mm Acoustic Holes For Bass
Wavelength Attenuation Spaced
900mm On Center

R   Concentric H-Section Aluminum
Channels 30mm Deep

S   Fiber Optic Cable

T   Perforated Metal Acoustic Panels
Painted Matte Putty-Grey
Insulated With 25mm Angel Hair
Fiberglass Acoustic Insulation

U   Mirrored Plexiglass Escutcheon
6mm Thick

V   3-Point Star

W   5-Point Star

X   7-Point Star

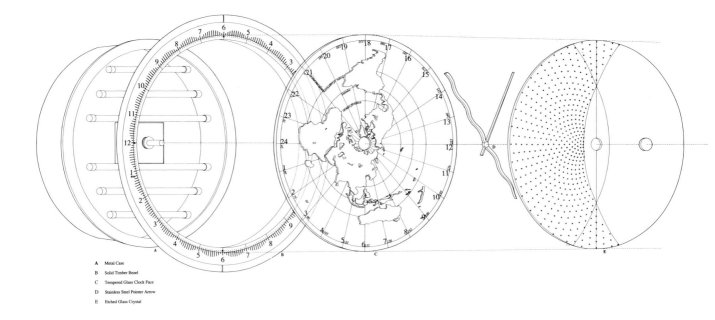

A   Metal Case

B   Solid Timber Bezel

C   Tempered Glass Clock Face

D   Stainless Steel Pointer Arrow

E   Etched Glass Crystal

hemisphere. The stars are represented by 723 fiber-optic points which match the light intensity, brilliance, color, and location of every first, second, and third magnitude star in the southern hemisphere's sky. Reinterpreted from mariners' astronomical charts, the entire hemisphere was proportionally contracted and transposed on the curved ceiling surface by placing a parallax-corrected, computer-drawn map on a flat temporary scaffolding deck, and plotting the position of every star on the ceiling with a plumb bob.

Appearing as they do to the naked eye, the various intensities of the stars are created by threading either single fiber-optic cables or bundles of two or four through perforations drilled in the ceiling. Illuminated by ten 150-watt metal halide sources contained in Australian-made light boxes which control the fiber optics' infra-red and ultra-violet rays, the fiber-optic stars are also distinguished by three distinct star-shaped escutcheons that correspond to their magnitude as typically represented on mariner's maps. The escutcheons, either 3-, 5- or 7-pointed, are made of a piece of metallic film laminated between two layers of acrylic (one clear and the other smoked), and produce a mirrored effect. The light quality of the stars is further modulated by an induced twinkle, generated by a series of motor-driven rotating paddles. The paddles are randomly positioned in a wheel located between the light source and the fibers to intermittently interrupt the light flow to the fibers. The light intensity is also periodically dimmed via a rotating mechanical vane—the final element producing the effect of a true night sky.

Detail Two: Clock
A focal point on the Star Court's west Comblanchien limestone wall is a backlighted "global clock." An extension of the celestial ceiling both as a space/time metaphor and in terms of its lighting effects, this decorative fixture adds to the storytelling quality of the space.

Designed as a light sculpture, the 5-foot-7-inch-diameter clock is a patent-pending, custom-designed chronometer which tells the sidereal time in all the

world's major cities. An elaborate construction depicting a polar equidistant map of the world, the clock represents 700 cities and has two hands—one of them fixed on Sydney, and the other moveable so that the time in any of the other cities can also be determined.

The clock is made from an etched-glass crystal studded on one side with a night canopy, an etched glass face topped with stainless-steel-plate cut-outs of the continents, a solid Tasmanian Blackwood bezel ring depicting the 24 hours of the day, a frosted Plexiglas diffuser, and a metal case containing several fluorescent light tubes. The world's cities, like the stars in the domed ceiling, are drilled into the continents on the clock's face and plugged with clear

quartz fibers so that when lighted from behind, each one is illuminated. Attached to a motor, the face rotates counter-clockwise once every 24 hours, while the shaded side of the etched-glass crystal graphically shows whether it is night or day in any particular city.

Six standard 36- and 18-watt fluorescent lamps of different lengths are surface-mounted to a 1/8-inch-thick enameled steel plate, bolted to the back of the light box with four Allen head screws. The interior of the light box is painted white to reflect the light, and the Plexiglas diffuser in front of it ensures an even distribution of light on the clock face. The lamps are accessed for maintenance from a special corridor built behind the clock.

Star Court

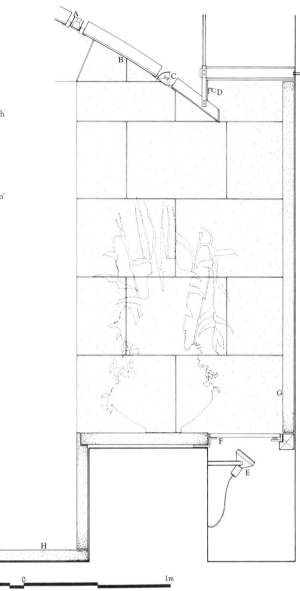

A   Recessed Accent Downlight With
     50W Dicrylic Bulbs

B   Curved Fibrous Plaster Ceiling With
     Perforations

C   Retractable Recessed Downlight
     With 50W Dicrylic Bulbs

D   12mm Linear Exposed Surface
     Mounted Neon Light

E   Bracket Mounted 'Permaflood Beam'
     Uplight

F   Glass Cover Plate

G   Limestone Cladding

H   Limestone Flooring

0.5   0   1m

Detail Three: Knuckle Niche

The Star Court connects to the adjacent office tower through a vestibule. Also in the form of an equilateral triangle, the vestibule serves as an architectural extension of the court itself. In its corners are niches, each of which contains a raised platform for showcasing a potted flower arrangement. The detailing of the niches echoes that of the Star Court: wedge-shaped, clad in Comblanchien limestone, and topped by a curved ceiling tapering to a handkerchief vault point. They also feature integrated lighting elements that enhance their overall effect. As in the Star Court, the lighting in the niches is predominantly reflected. The effect is achieved with three primary components: two recessed halogen downlights, which directly light the flowers; a concealed PAR 38 uplight hidden below the platform, which silhouettes the flower arrangement; and a concealed neon tube in the ceiling valence, which washes the upper portion of the stone wall and floats the vaulted ceiling.

All of the lighting was selected for the single purpose of presenting the flower arrangement as a centerpiece. The white halogen sources were selected for their high color-rendering capability. Above the flowers, the recessed 50-watt lamp, which is retractable to allow for the ceiling slope, provides an adjustable, narrowly focused beam on the arrangement. Dichroic fittings add key lighting to the flowers to bring out their vibrant colors. At 3,000 degrees Kelvin, the neon was chosen to match the color rendering properties of the white light of the halogens. Surface-mounted to the structural system suspending the vault, the linear neon not only softly washes the warm limestone wall behind the flowers, highlighting its inherent gold and wine-colored markings, but calls further attention to the vault pointing toward the flowers and raises the level of illumination within the niche. Bracket-mounted to the wall in a recessed pocket below and behind the platform, a single 100-watt PAR 38 halogen flood lamp throws a broad wash of light up behind the flowers. The pocket is covered with a sheet of 1/2-inch-thick glass, which cools the warm light of the PAR lamp before it reaches the wall surface.

Star Court

Detail Four: Pitchi Lamps

Another decorative fixture in the Star Court is what the architects call the "pitchi lamp." Thirteen of these fixtures, centered in front of columns that define the perimeter of the court, function as point sources for reading and as warm backlights that silhouette potted blue palms. Enhancing the story of Australian culture told through architectural forms, these fixtures adapt the Aboriginal *pitchi*—a carved bowl used as everything from a shovel or spade to a bassinet or serving dish—for use as a lamp shade.

Each lamp is composed of a 4-foot-high, 4-legged quadruped base supporting two 1/4-inch-thick pitchi-inspired glass diffusers. A standard incandescent 60-watt A lamp is sandwiched between the glass diffusers, while three stainless-steel louver rings between the diffusers shield the lamp from direct view. The slump-cast diffusers are made of "Starglaze" clear glass, notable for its low iron content and subsequent lack of green tint. They are etched with a pattern reminiscent of mythological carvings on Aboriginal bowls and sand-blasted on the inside. A steel release pin positions the diffusers into place, and is pulled to allow them to slip out for access to the lamp. A decorative stainless-steel pull-cord with a stainless plumb bob turns the lamp on and off. Power is fed through a concealed channel in one leg, and the electrical cord is looped through a hole in a 1-inch-thick stone base to an outlet in the floor. The lighting load for the entire Star Court is approximately 2.1 watts/foot.

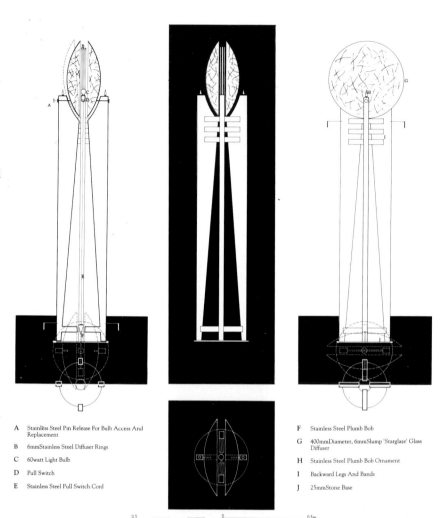

A	Stainless Steel Pin Release For Bulb Access And Replacement
B	6mm Stainless Steel Diffuser Rings
C	60 watt Light Bulb
D	Pull Switch
E	Stainless Steel Pull Switch Cord

F	Stainless Steel Plumb Bob
G	400mm Diameter, 6mm Slump 'Starglaze' Glass Diffuser
H	Stainless Steel Plumb Bob Ornament
I	Backward Legs And Bands
J	25mm Stone Base

INSTITUTIONAL

DAVID SAUL SMITH UNION, BOWDOIN COLLEGE

Location: Brunswick, Maine

Interior Architect: Hardy Holzman Pfeiffer Associates

Lighting Designer: Hardy Holzman Pfeiffer Associates

Manufacturers: Michael's Lighting (metal work); Osram/Sylvania (compact fluorescents); Motorola (ballasts).

Date Completed: March 1995

Photography: Brian Vanden Brink

Renovated by architects Hardy Holzman Pfeiffer Associates, the David Saul Smith student union at Bowdoin College—originally designed as a gymnasium in 1912 by Allens and Collins—is a vivacious medley of color and form with boldly patterned walls, a vast yellow linoleum floor inlaid with a 90-foot rendition of the school's seal, furniture upholstered in bright floral prints, and a circular ramp surrounded by a scalloped wall. Enhancing the playful atmosphere are custom lighting elements—most notably a series of lighted columns defining the circulation ramp, which wraps

around the space and leads to a series of smaller spaces on the floor above.

While the double-height space is primarily illuminated during the day with natural light streaming through clerestory windows, at night general illumination is provided by 23 custom pendants suspended from the 46-foot-high ceiling and fitted with metal halide lamps. The columns lining the ramp, while essentially decorative, complement the light from the sunlike domes with additional illumination diffused through their fanlike tops. Positioned in pairs, the lighted columns accentuate the ramp's upward movement, and in some cases mark the entrance to the additional spaces—including a bookstore, a pub, a cafe, and gallery and lounge areas—that shoot off it along the way.

Each column is constructed of a 10-foot-high aluminum pole topped by a V-shaped perforated aluminum diffuser, whose scalloped edges echo the undulating wall surrounding the ramp. To be sure that the diffusers wouldn't "oil

can," a condition in which the aluminum tends to curl, engineers from Michael's Lighting who collaborated on the project specified a heavy 14-gauge aluminum. They also specified that the perforated panels be 40 percent open to allow the proper amount of light to shine through. The diffusers are sandblasted and finished with a clear coat of urethane, then baked at 140 degrees by short wave infrared lamps to give them a longer life.

Two 40-watt compact warm-white fluorescents are mounted at 40-degree angles in a custom mounting device between the panels of the 6-foot-wide diffuser. The lamps are wired from the floor through the pole with remote electronic ballasts mounted in the columns' pedestals. To diffuse the light further, each lamp is individually wrapped, like a cigar, with an additional 14-gauge sheet of perforated aluminum. Because Maine gets chilly and gloomy in the colder months, the lamps were chosen for their warm color as well as for their energy efficiency.

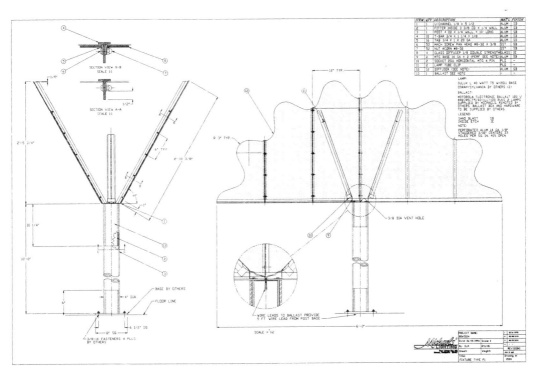

DEPARTMENT OF ART AND ARCHEOLOGY, McCORMIC HALL, PRINCETON UNIVERSITY

Location: Princeton, New Jersey

Interior Architect: Ford, Farewell, Mills and Gatsch, Architects

Lighting Designer: Michael Farewell, Gonzalo Rizo-Patron

Manufacturers: SPI (Echo quartz uplight); Times Square (projector Q250 downlight); Blue Line Fabricators (stainless-steel rods); Pinkus (tempered glass); Echo (assembly).

Date Completed: January 1993

Photography: Chuck Choi

In their renovation of the department of art and archeology at Princeton University, architects Ford, Farewell, Mills and Gatsch devised a composition of two contrasting types of spaces for the department's different functions. Located in a contemporary building, the department consists of lounge areas, classrooms, and auditorium spaces, all of which the architects defined with modern, free-flowing forms, and general office areas, which were developed as more traditional spaces. To emphasize the difference between these two types

of spaces, the architects designed a custom light fixture which projects an image of the building's plan onto the floor in the entry corridor linking both parts of the building.

A play on the idea of the art historian who compares and contrasts works of art with a double slide projector, the light fixture is itself a kind of mock projector fitted with a tin stencil of the building's plan, which, when projected onto the floor, graphically illustrates the difference in the spaces. In addition to setting the tone for the department and functioning as an orientation map, the image also serves as an aesthetic grounding element in the context of the space, like a work of art or quasi-floorcovering in the center of the open lounge area beneath a large, circular ceiling oculus. The lighting fixture also highlights the oculus and provides general ambient illumination for the space.

In keeping with the modernist aesthetic established in this area, the fixture is composed of four hooded reflector uplights surrounding a single pro-

jector downlight, which is concealed in a black-painted cylindrical aluminum housing. The uplights are mounted to a square aluminum ring, which also supports the downlight, and the entire assembly is suspended from the ceiling by 3/8-inch-diameter stainless-steel rods. Each uplight element consists of a 100-watt linear quartz lamp contained within a standard reflector to allow for uniform illumination of the white ceiling oculus, which reflects the light back into the space. Beneath the 250-watt projector lamp in the fixture's central housing is a round plate of clear tempered glass, 2 feet in diameter, which serves as a lens for the fixture and echoes the form of the oculus. The stainless-steel rods penetrate through holes in the plate and are fixed into place with acorn cap nuts. Slots in the housing allow the stenciled floor plan to slide into place. The projected image is approximately 8 feet in length and more or less matches the diameter of the ceiling oculus.

Because it also functions as an exhibit area, the architects chose to illu-

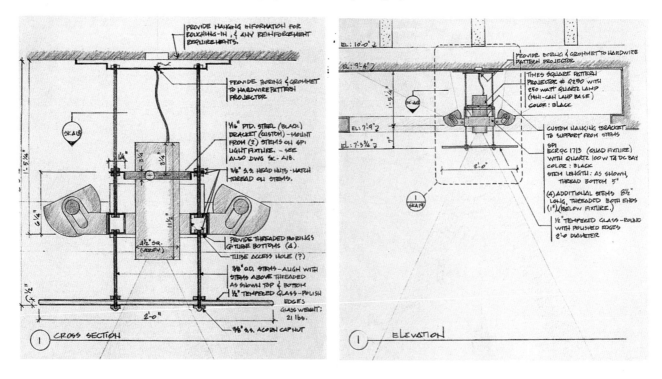

CROSS SECTION

ELEVATION

minate the space primarily with indirect lighting, selecting quartz lamps for their white light and high color-rendering characteristics. The fixture is connected to a dimmer, which raises or lowers the level of light depending on the time of day, since daylight also permeates the space through south-facing windows. Other low-voltage track lights provide accent light along the walls when localized wall washing is demanded for art exhibitions.

MICHAEL C. CARLOS MUSEUM, EMORY UNIVERSITY

Location: Atlanta, Georgia

Architect: Michael Graves, Architect

Lighting Designer: Douglas Baker

Manufacturers: Philips (fluorescent lamps); Lithonia and C.J. Lighting (fluorescent fixtures); Benjamin Moore (paint, interior cove surface); P.S.G. (custom chandelier and sconces).

Date Completed: May 1993

Photography: Steven Brooke

The architecture of Emory University's Michael C. Carlos Museum in Atlanta, designed by the firm of architect Michael Graves, was partly inspired by the museum's collection of Greek, Roman, Egyptian, and ancient Near East antiquities. In the museum's public spaces, contemporary, abstract interpretations of classical architectural elements—such as large-scale symmetrical portals which suggest heavy stone column and lintel construction—establish an appropriate contextual prelude for the art. Because the exhibition spaces are quieter rooms architecturally, the lobbies provided an opportunity to introduce character, variety, and color into the museum experience. Lighting, too, plays a key role in accentuating the character of the architecture in one of the most visible public spaces, a lobby area leading to a large lecture and banquet hall. There, an abstraction of a classic colonnade, expressed by a row of clerestory colonnettes along two sides of the room, is highlighted with integrated cove lighting and custom faux bronze and alabaster chandeliers and sconces that recall antique oil lamps or candle sconces.

Created in conjunction with lighting designer Douglas Baker, the cove light and fixtures were designed to emulate the mood of dimly lit, classical settings. The

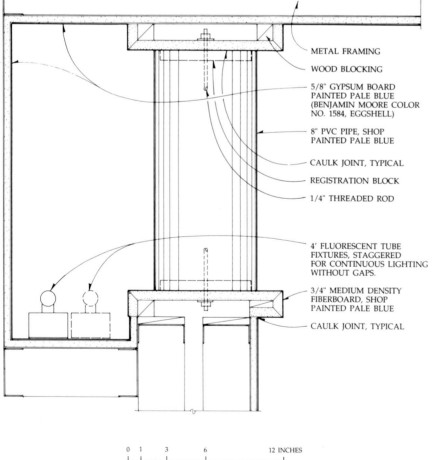

METAL FRAMING

WOOD BLOCKING

5/8" GYPSUM BOARD PAINTED PALE BLUE (BENJAMIN MOORE COLOR NO. 1584, EGGSHELL)

8" PVC PIPE, SHOP PAINTED PALE BLUE

CAULK JOINT, TYPICAL

REGISTRATION BLOCK

1/4" THREADED ROD

4' FLUORESCENT TUBE FIXTURES, STAGGERED FOR CONTINUOUS LIGHTING WITHOUT GAPS.

3/4" MEDIUM DENSITY FIBERBOARD, SHOP PAINTED PALE BLUE

CAULK JOINT, TYPICAL

0 1   3   6   12 INCHES

SECTION THROUGH LIGHT COVE

fluorescent light emanating from the cove behind the clerestorylike colonnette creates the illusion of daylight in the windowless room, while dimmed warmer incandescent A lamps and bent-tip, clear, candelabra-base sources in the sconces and chandeliers suggest candlelight.

Running the entire length of the 75-foot-long hall, staggered fluorescents concealed within the 1-foot-wide-by-2-foot-deep cove create a continuous band of diffuse light behind the colonnades. The fluorescent light reflects off the interior drywall surface of the cove, which is painted a matte pale blue, before hitting the colonnades, whose truncated 18-inch-high columns are constructed of PVC pipes and also painted pale blue. More flattering to a patron's skin tone, the incandescent light of the sconces and chandeliers also enhance the warmer finishes and materials used in this space, including the pearwood doors, bronze fixtures, and Etowah pink, gray, and white Georgian marble floor.

As all of the light sources in the space are on independent dimmers, they can be adjusted to various levels for different events.

OHRSTROM LIBRARY, ST. PAUL'S SCHOOL

Location: Concord, New Hampshire

Architect: Robert A.M. Stern Architects

Lighting Designer: Cline Bettridge Bernstein Lighting Design, Inc.

Manufacturers: Bergen Art Metal

Date Completed: January 1991

Photography: Peter Aaron/ESTO

Dotting the villagelike campus of the St. Paul's School, a traditional New England boarding school in Concord, New Hampshire, are a collection of buildings dating back as far as 1859. Inspired by James Gamble Rogers' nearby 1937 School House, the school's Ohrstrom Library, designed by architect Robert A.M. Stern Architects, is characterized by red brick and Briar Hill stone facades and interior oak panelling intended to evoke the traditional spirit of its neigh-

bors. The attention to detailing reinforcing this Ivy League atmosphere was such that the architects designed custom light fixtures reminiscent of the past, demanding in addition that their illumination recall the warm light of an earlier era. Modern light levels and energy codes precluded the use of incandescent sources, however, so with assistance from lighting designers Cline Bettridge Bernstein the architects developed a family of fixtures which incorporate compact fluorescent fixtures while simulating the warmth of incandescent illumination.

The basic building block of the fixtures is an 8-inch-diameter glass cylinder, which houses a compact fluorescent lamp and ballast. The cylinders are used singularly or in pairs, as wall sconces or grouped in circles of 6, 8, or 16, and are also employed as ceiling pendants. Col-

lectively they provide the required level of 30 footcandles of ambient or task illumination for study carrels, book stacks, and desk and seating areas (custom table and floor lamps provide additional light where needed). Using mock-ups with different glass and theatrical gels, the lighting designers found a color which, when permeated with the light of the compact fluorescents, matched the light of incandescents. They used the information derived from their experiments to develop a custom translucent enamel which was applied to the glass used in the fixtures. So convincing is the color that even the camera used to take the image shown on the facing page was fooled.

Developed in different sizes to illuminate the smaller reading rooms and intimately scaled niches as well as the larger two-story-high main reading

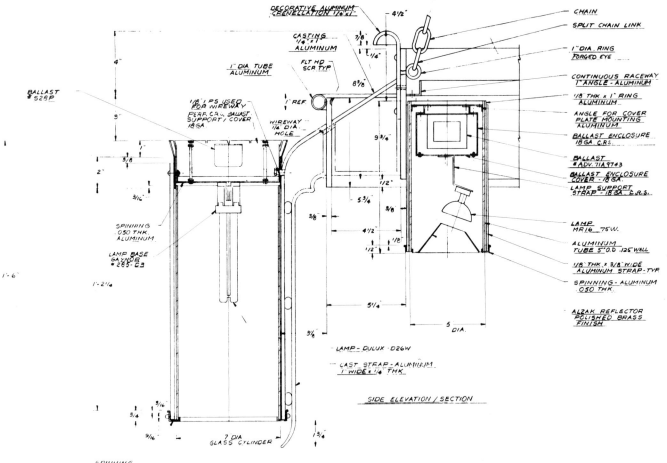

room with appropriate levels of diffuse ambient light, the pendants are elaborately detailed with blackened steel molding and crenellations, brass crowns and base rings. The larger chandeliers, suspended by blackened steel chains from the vaulted ceiling of the main reading room, also contain a less conspicuous inner ring of 75-watt MR-16 or 150-watt PAR 38 downlights. Housed within blackened steel cylinders, which also conceal transformers, the downlights are either angled at 15 degrees through brass reflector cones to punch focused accent lighting toward specific reading areas or aimed straight down for direct light over the tables.

All of the fixtures use the same size compact fluorescent source, which was selected for its long life of 10,000 hours, ease of maintenance, and high lumen output. The three pendants in the main reading room illuminate the space at fewer than 2 watts/square foot.

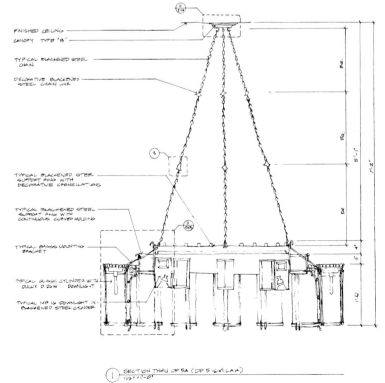

TOWELL LIBRARY, UCLA

Location: Los Angeles, California

Architect: Hodgetts+Fung Design Associates

Interior Architect: Hodgetts+Fung Design Associates

Electrical Engineer: Patrick Byrne and Associates

Lighting Consultant: Patrick Quigley and Associates

Manufacturers: Up- and downlight struts: Unistrut (struts); Day-Brite/Benjamin (400-watt HID high bay metal halides); Prudential (fluorescents). Study carrel strip lights: Prudential (fluorescents). Exterior reading lanterns: Hubble (500-watt quartz flood lamp); Glasteel (corrugated fiberglass reflector).

Date Completed: September 1992

Photography: Ken Naverson

Detail One: Up- and Downlights

Hodgetts+Fung Design Associates brought the humblest materials to the loftiest levels in a temporary library structure for the University of California, Los Angeles. While at $83 per square foot the budget was limited, the architects' imaginations were not, a fact best exhibited in their ability to turn standard, off-the-shelf fixtures and materials into integrated extensions of their design concept.

Two examples of the holistic approach to lighting appear in the main reading room, a tentlike structure supported by aluminum ribs extending like spokes from a central core and covered by a taut polyvinyl and foam-laminate skin. The first is a series of up- and downlights attached to cantilevered struts extending from the central core, the second a group of direct fluorescent strip lights that provide task illumination for the study carrels positioned around the perimeter of the structure.

The uplight fixtures emphasize the height of the structure; provide ambient, diffuse fill light for the space so that the structure appears evenly lit and glows like a lantern from the outside; and reduces the contrast between the interior spaces covered by translucent panels and those darker areas covered by opaque panels. These goals were accomplished by attaching standard 400-watt high intensity discharge high bay metal halides to the ends of the struts, which are bolted to the aluminum ribs. The struts are supported by galvanized aircraft cables and extend at an 8-foot radius from the aluminum ribs. They are positioned above eye level at a height of 8 feet and the ambient light from the metal halide fixtures is reflected off the white surface of the polyvinyl panels.

The positioning of the fluorescent downlights mounted below the struts was also critical. Because the budget limited the use of fixture shielding and baffles, the T-12 cool white fluorescent fixtures are equipped with metal reflectors and are oriented to flank the carrels around the central hub to minimize reflected glare at the worksurface.

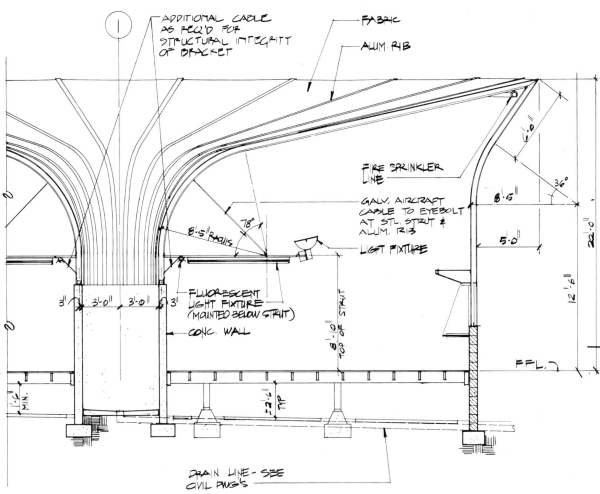

ADDITIONAL CABLE AS REQ'D FOR STRUCTURAL INTEGRITY OF BRACKET

FABRIC

ALUM. RIB

FIRE SPRINKLER LINE

GALV. AIRCRAFT CABLE TO EYEBOLT AT STL. STRUT & ALUM. RIB

LIGHT FIXTURE

8'-5" RADIUS

78°

36°

6'-0"

8'-5"

5'-0"

22'-0"

12'-6"

FLUORESCENT LIGHT FIXTURE (MOUNTED BELOW STRUT)

CONC. WALL

3" 3'-0" 3'-0" 3"

8'-0" TOP OF STRUT

FFL

±2'-6" TYP

MIN.

DRAIN LINE - SEE CIVIL DWG'S

Towell Library

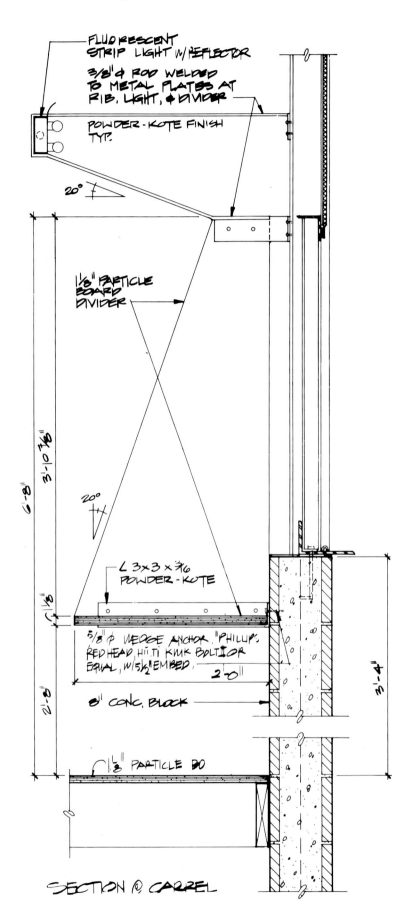

FLUORESCENT STRIP LIGHT W/ REFLECTOR

3/8"ø ROD WELDED TO METAL PLATES AT RIB, LIGHT, & DIVIDER

POWDER-KOTE FINISH TYP.

20°

1 1/8" PARTICLE BOARD DIVIDER

20°

L 3x3x3/16 POWDER-KOTE

5/8"ø WEDGE ANCHOR "PHILLIPS RED HEAD, HILTI KWIK BOLT II OR EQUAL, W/5 1/2" EMBED

8" CONC. BLOCK

1 1/8" PARTICLE BD

6'-8"

3'-10 7/8"

2'-0"

2'-0"

3'-4"

SECTION @ CARREL

Detail Two: Task Lighting

The fluorescent strip lights providing task illumination for the study carrels around the perimeter of the library's reading room are also positioned to minimize glare. Though they are placed parallel to the worksurfaces—which is less ideal than the perpendicular placement of the downlights attached to the struts around the core—the two T-12 strip lights are cantilevered from the wall and positioned over and behind the user to reduce indirect glare. They also balance the lighting conditions created by a ribbon of windows facing the carrels.

By making the fixtures architecturally significant, the eye is tricked into forgiv-

ing the glare where it isn't completely avoidable. Appearing as though floating in space, the fluorescent strip lights are attached to a frame that also supports the worksurface. The frame consists of two bent metal rods (evocative of Eames furniture) welded to metal plates that are connected to 1/8-inch-thick particle board dividers and bolted to the aluminum ribs. The fluorescent strip lights are mounted to a solid fascia inserted in the squared angle of the bent metal rods, which cantilever 2 feet out from the wall. They are also equipped with reflectors to avoid exposing the bare lamp to the eye. A Powder Kote finish on the rods and metal plates aid in reducing reflectivity.

The compound system of ambient uplight and direct downlight provides the appropriate, varied light levels needed to successfully illuminate the space while also addressing color, an important element in the original lighting concept. The cool light from the uplights was intended to recede, while the downlights were to be equipped with warmer sources to flatter human features, providing a more social context and contrasting with the cool uplights. Though the budget initially prohibited the use of warmer fluorescents, with the new Federal Energy policy in effect, the downlights should be replaced with appropriate high color rendering lamps, fulfilling the original lighting design concept.

Since the temporary library was an institutional project, it was not bound by California's strict energy standards. Nevertheless, the lighting systems employed in the space are highly efficient, consuming only 2 watts per square foot by night and 1.24 watts per square foot by day, compared to the 2.25 watts per square foot allowed under these codes. While sophisticated controls were cost prohibitive, the circuitry was designed to be manually switched in sections to make efficient use of the daylight penetrating the translucent panels of the building's skin.

OFFICE

ACKERMAN McQUEEN

Location: Tulsa, Oklahoma

Interior Architect: Elliott+Associates Architects

Lighting Designer: Elliott+Associates Architects with Phil Easlon of Hunszicker Brothers

Manufacturers: Light Tower: Halo (MR-16 lamps); Robinson Glass (etched glass, acrylic angles); Braekel Millwork (wood trim); Diversified Construction (drywall); Sherwin Williams (paint); Buysse Electric (electrical contractor); Lassiter-Richey Construction (general contractor). Light slot: Mettalux (fluorescent lamps); Robinson Glass (acrylic lens); Braekel Millwork (wood trim); Diversified Construction (drywall); Sherwin Williams (paint); Sun Dial Painting (wallcovering); Lassiter-Richey Construction (general contractor).

Date Completed: July 1993

Photography: Bob Shimer/Hedrich-Blessing

Detail One: Light Towers

Architect Rand Elliott developed an aesthetic around the abstract notion of being on the inside of an idea, giving form to glimmers of inspiration that are cleverly manifested in his use of light. Ackerman McQueen's offices are characterized by poured-in-place concrete structural columns, 12-, 14-, and 18-foot ceiling heights, and walls punctuated by clerestory and porthole windows. The columns and layers of space, shaped in part by the variations in ceiling heights, inspired two compelling lighting details.

The most dramatic of many sources are a series of 12 custom floor-to-ceiling "light towers." First seen from a low-ceilinged, serpentine passage, the towers appear as slender slots of receding light punctuating the outer sheetrocked wall of a high-ceilinged conference room. These bursts of light evolve into tangible form inside the conference room where they protrude into the space and offer explosive emphasis on the verticality of this 18-foot-high volume. Lining the walls at 6-foot intervals, the towers are 18-foot-high by 7⅛-inch-wide rectangular shafts that vary from 12 to 18 inches in depth and are composed of three panes of 1/4-inch etched glass, sealed at the corners with clear silicone and reinforced with clear acrylic angles for support. One side of each shaft is left open to create the recess seen from the outside.

Each tower is fitted with two standard low-voltage fixtures with 50-watt

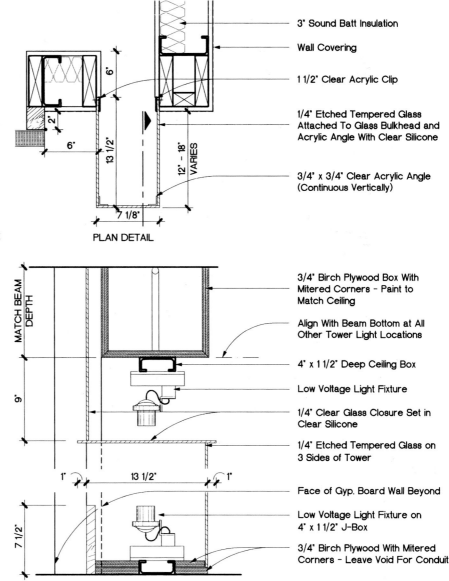

PLAN DETAIL

- 3" Sound Batt Insulation
- Wall Covering
- 1 1/2" Clear Acrylic Clip
- 1/4" Etched Tempered Glass Attached To Glass Bulkhead and Acrylic Angle With Clear Silicone
- 3/4" x 3/4" Clear Acrylic Angle (Continuous Vertically)

VERTICAL SECTION

- 3/4" Birch Plywood Box With Mitered Corners - Paint to Match Ceiling
- Align With Beam Bottom at All Other Tower Light Locations
- 4" x 1 1/2" Deep Ceiling Box
- Low Voltage Light Fixture
- 1/4" Clear Glass Closure Set in Clear Silicone
- 1/4" Etched Tempered Glass on 3 Sides of Tower
- Face of Gyp. Board Wall Beyond
- Low Voltage Light Fixture on 4" x 1 1/2" J-Box
- 3/4" Birch Plywood With Mitered Corners - Leave Void For Conduit

very narrow spot MR-16 lamps emitting enough light to penetrate the entire volume of the shafts so that, from inside the conference room, they appear to be solid blocks of diffused light. One of these fixtures is mounted to the floor, protected and hidden from view in the recess by a 7½-inch-high baseboard of painted plywood, and can be accessed through the open space rising above it. Two blocks of 3/4-inch-thick plywood are stacked on either side of the junction box allowing a conduit to be surface-mounted above the floor to avoid the need to core drill the floor for access to power. The fixture emits a whitish light towards the slender slot on the outer wall, and a yellow-orange light toward the conference room. The close proximity of the etched glass allows the UV light to touch it and create a band of color at the base of the tower. In contrast to the aqua cast of the rest of the column, the yellow band of light creates a hot-spot that calls attention to the bottom edge of the volume.

The other fixture is mounted either to a ceiling beam with a surface-mounted conduit or to a 6-inch-deep plywood box with mitered corners. The boxes contain the conduit and equal the depth of the beams so that each fixture is mounted at a consistent height. By enclosing the ceiling-mounted fixtures with a pocket of clear glass, rather than the etched glass facing the remainder of the column, they appear like halos of light in ethereal contrast to the black-painted ceiling. A plate of 1/4-inch-thick clear glass, placed on top of the light column 15 inches below the ceiling, supports three other panes of clear glass that create the clear pocket housing the fixture. The glass enclosure maintains acoustical privacy in the conference room yet its back side is left open for access to the low-voltage fixture.

Detail Two: Light Shafts

Another light detail appears in shorter shafts of light surrounding the outer side of a 9- to 10-foot-high, sloping, U-shaped wall enclosing the serpentine passage to the conference room. Unlike

the light towers, however, these smaller-scale shafts are embedded within the wall rather than receding into or protruding from it. Seen from the office area, the light shafts offer fill light in the hallway and presage the taller light towers on the outside wall of the conference room, which can be seen at certain angles in the approach from the office area.

The six small-scale shafts, placed at 8-foot intervals around the wall, are fitted with standard 40-watt, two-lamp fluorescent fixtures that are color-corrected to emit a whiter light. The fixture is contained between two 5½-inch-

deep metals studs faced with two layers of 1/4-inch-thick molded, fabric-covered dry wall on the inside of the wall. The metal studs buffer the light fixture from 3-inch-thick sound batt insulation within the wall structure, which is also faced with two layers of 1/4-inch-thick dry wall on the outer wall. The outer wall is painted in a matte blue-green color and amplifies the effect of the natural light pouring in through the skylight and porthole windows in other areas of the space.

The 9-inch-wide-by-5-inch-deep-by-9-foot-tall pockets containing the fixtures are faced on the outer wall with a

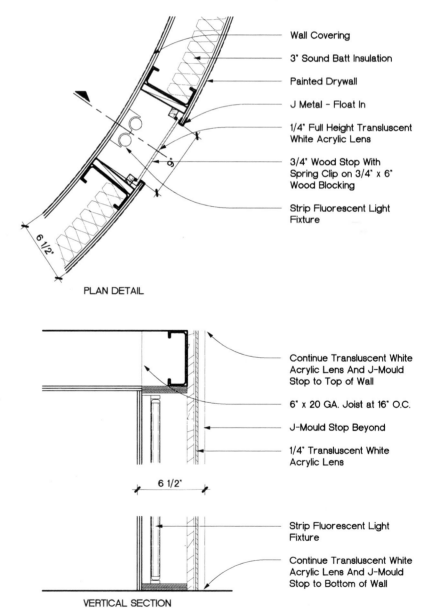

PLAN DETAIL

Wall Covering

3" Sound Batt Insulation

Painted Drywall

J Metal - Float In

1/4" Full Height Transluscent White Acrylic Lens

3/4" Wood Stop With Spring Clip on 3/4" x 6" Wood Blocking

Strip Fluorescent Light Fixture

Continue Transluscent White Acrylic Lens And J-Mould Stop to Top of Wall

6" x 20 GA. Joist at 16" O.C.

J-Mould Stop Beyond

1/4" Transluscent White Acrylic Lens

Strip Fluorescent Light Fixture

Continue Transluscent White Acrylic Lens And J-Mould Stop to Bottom of Wall

VERTICAL SECTION

translucent, 1/4-inch-thick acrylic lens that diffuses the light. The lens is held in place between two 3/4-inch-thick plinths and four metal spring clips which may be snapped out, allowing the lens to be removed for access to the

lamps. A shadowy version of the bands of light at the tops and bottoms of the light towers is created in the smaller-scale light shafts in this wall by extending the lens to the full height of the wall, which rests on and is topped with

6-inch-high, 20-gauge steel joists. A gap is left between the translucent lens and the areas above and below the fixtures to allow for heat distribution and the emission of a ghostly glow of light on the tops and bottoms of the shafts.

D.E. Shaw

Location: New York, New York

Interior Designer: Steven Holl
Architect

Manufacturers: Tom Jenkinson
(in-house technical consultant); Hand
Fabrication (custom metal fixtures);
Clark Construction (project contractor);
Schiller Decorator Co. (painting
contractor); Ron-glo (paint); Lightolier
(electrical fittings).

Date Completed: November 1991

Photography: Paul Warchol

The eerie emanations of colored light
issuing from behind the notched walls
in the offices of D.E. Shaw & Co. may
seem more appropriate on a sci-fi movie
set than in the entrance lobby of a
financial analysis firm. But the relevance
of architect Steven Holl's mysterious
lighting scheme becomes apparent when
you consider both the cutting-edge, if
obscure, financial instruments D.E.
Shaw's computer whizzes study and the
state-of-the-art technology that drives
these financial analysts' activities.

   The futuristic aspect of D.E. Shaw's
work—namely, interpreting the minus-
cule spreads of global securities for an
elite group of high finance investors—is
baffling to even the most experienced
Wall Street pros. Reflecting the company's progressive image, Holl's unusual
design of gaps and fissures, accentuated
with unseen sources of exotic light, provides a fitting design metaphor for the
client's curious and intangible business
program. As difficult as the light may be
to comprehend on the surface, however,
the design concept is actually very simple: daylight and fluorescent lamps
combined with reflective materials.

   Located on the top two floors of a
midtown Manhattan skyscraper, D.E.
Shaw's offices are exposed to plenty of
natural light during the day. Holl's
design for the reception lobby blocks
most of it, however, with an interior
drywall system that virtually covers the
windows on the north wall. Carved and
notched in ad hoc configurations, the
wall system allows only a small amount
of daylight into the 31-square-foot
lobby space. By painting the back sides

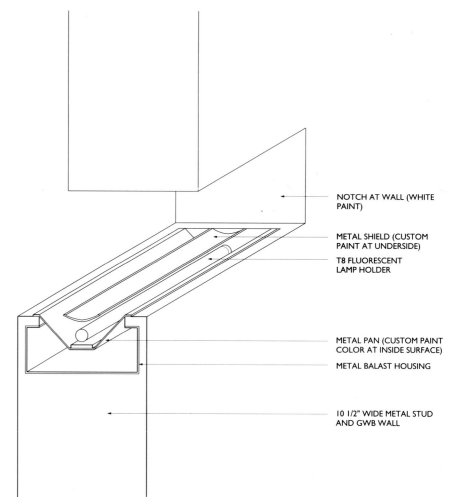

NOTCH AT WALL (WHITE
PAINT)

METAL SHIELD (CUSTOM
PAINT AT UNDERSIDE)

T8 FLUORESCENT
LAMP HOLDER

METAL PAN (CUSTOM PAINT
COLOR AT INSIDE SURFACE)

METAL BALAST HOUSING

10 1/2" WIDE METAL STUD
AND GWB WALL

DISNEY ANIMATION BUILDING

Location: Burbank, California

Architect: Robert A.M. Stern Architects

Lighting Designer: Cosentini Lighting

Manufacturers: Translite Systems, Jim Prior (fixtures); Osram (AR-70s).

Date Completed: December 1994

Photography: Peter Aaron/ESTO

In response to the enormous success in the 1980s of the Walt Disney Company's feature animation films, Roy Disney, Walt's nephew and head of Disney's animation division, decided one building was needed for the 700 animators whose studios were dispersed throughout Glendale, California. Designed by Robert A.M. Stern Architects, the new building was inspired in part by the architecture of the original animation studios designed by early modernist architect Kem Weber, who developed the master plan for Disney's Burbank facilities in 1939. The architects updated the building by combining its early modern style with their own lively, thematic narrative. One of the most imaginative elements is an elaborate chandelier suspended in Roy Disney's office.

The office is located in a 60-foot-tall cone, which, from the exterior, marks the building's entrance and is meant to suggest Mickey Mouse's magician's hat from the feature animation film "Fantasia." Expressions of the stars and moons adorning the hat are featured in both the furniture and lighting elements. A custom-designed desk takes the shape of a moon, for instance, while the central chandelier—a construction of light-studded, overlapping circular rings—creates a starry constellation of abstracted Mickey Mouse faces when viewed in plan.

The chandelier was developed serendipitously, resulting from a change in the office's design during construction. The architects had planned to suspend a flat ceiling within the cone-shaped room, but realized that by allowing the space to rise to its full height a much more dramatic effect could be created. The 20-foot-diameter office was designed to double as a meeting space. Therefore the lighting needed to be comfortable enough for Roy Disney to work in, and at the same time accentuate the architectural volume and illuminate the lounge area for press interviews. The chandelier combines up- and downlighting and is connected to a programmable dimming system that allows it to be adjusted for various purposes.

Developed from standard nickel-plated brass components, the chandelier is constructed of 12 concentric low-voltage tubular tracks in two sizes, suspended at different heights with tin-plated wire from the ceiling. All 12 tracks support a series of 50-watt AR-70 fixtures—half of which are directed upward and the other half pointed down. Nine of the shielded filament Halo Star lamps are positioned on the larger rings and six on the smaller ones, providing true-to-color halogen light which consistently renders the room's dynamic color scheme. Complemented by daylight streaming through a circular skylight during the day and incandescent light from two Nessen torchieres, the lamps were chosen for their color, compact size, high light output levels, energy efficiency, and flexibility. Fitted with conical reflectors which recall the shape of the room, the pivoting lamps were adjusted to throw focused light on specific areas. The designers wanted as few cables as possible to support the fixture, so the mechanical and electrical supports were integrated to support and feed power to each 3-ring fixture, with six out of seven suspension cables supplying the current.

Powered by a remote transformer, with the secondary voltage calibrated to account for the dramatic height of the ceiling, the fixtures were mounted no higher than 15 feet above the floor for ease of maintenance. They are relamped every three years and provide a unique lighting solution at under 4 watts/square foot.

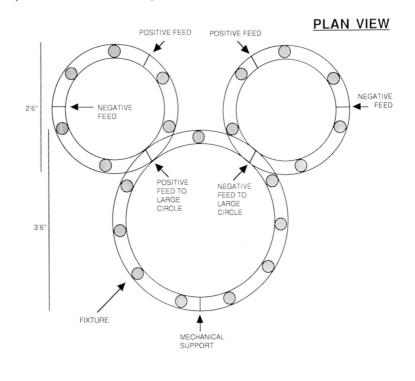

PLAN VIEW

POSITIVE FEED

POSITIVE FEED

NEGATIVE FEED

NEGATIVE FEED

2'6"

POSITIVE FEED TO LARGE CIRCLE

NEGATIVE FEED TO LARGE CIRCLE

3'6"

FIXTURE

MECHANICAL SUPPORT

BRIDGE CONFIGURATION AT CROSSOVER

UNINSULATED, TIN PLATED AWG#10 COPPER WIRE

TOP BRIDGE - NON-CONDUCTIVE

BOTTOM BRIDGE - FEEDS POWER TO ONE CONDUCTOR

ISOLATOR

EDGE

Location: New York, New York

Interior Architect: Peter Himmelstein Design

Lighting Designer: Peter Himmelstein Design

Manufacturers: T. Lee's Contracting (metal work); Philips (fluorescents and incandescents).

Date Completed: January 1994

Photography: Chuck Choi

When the managers of Outline Press Syndicate created a new division called Edge to represent a select group of photographers, they knew it needed to have a strong identity in order to stand out among the stiffly competitive photo agencies in New York. They commissioned architect Peter Himmelstein to make a design statement in its offices on lower Broadway that would establish it as a bold, exciting new-comer to the market. On a very limited budget, Himmelstein crafted a classic presence for the agency by developing crisp custom

interior features from stock elements and a limited palette of materials. The most dramatic feature is a custom light fixture which was developed to serve as the design statement's architectural exclamation point.

Aside from its role as a design highlight, the light fixture was designed to provide ambient illumination for virtually the entire space. Suspended from the ceiling, the 35-foot-long fixture runs along the length of the office over the six custom workstations used by the independent reps, metaphorically tying them together as a team. Echoing the painted steel frame and laminate glass door of the conference room and the painted steel and fluted glass dividers between the workstations, the light fixture is an extension of the materials palette. It is composed of a two-part painted steel frame inlaid with hand-sanded acrylic panels which diffuse the light of both fluorescent and incandescent sources. It is suspended by 12 threaded rods connected

to the structural steel inside the concrete ceiling. One portion of the frame runs parallel to the floor and supports an armature to which the light sources are mounted. The two-lamp, full spectrum fluorescents over the acrylic panels mounted to this portion of the frame illuminate the work surfaces of the stations below. Ten 75-watt PAR 38 incandescent flood lamps are positioned to project light through the acrylic panels on the second portion of the frame, which is angled toward the reception desk and production area where portfolios are assembled. The panels, 1½ by 6 feet on the horizontal part of the frame and 2 by 3 feet on the angled section, rest on angled steel clips. Flexible metal conduit extends from the ceiling to the fixture at one point to supply power to the whole fixture.

The incandescent and fluorescent sources are connected to separate switches and dimmers so that either can be turned on separately or together.

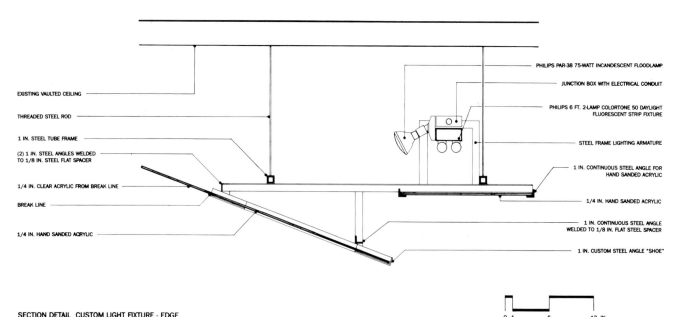

EXISTING VAULTED CEILING

THREADED STEEL ROD

1 IN. STEEL TUBE FRAME

(2) 1 IN. STEEL ANGLES WELDED
TO 1/8 IN. STEEL FLAT SPACER

1/4 IN. CLEAR ACRYLIC FROM BREAK LINE

BREAK LINE

1/4 IN. HAND SANDED ACRYLIC

PHILIPS PAR-38 75-WATT INCANDESCENT FLOODLAMP

JUNCTION BOX WITH ELECTRICAL CONDUIT

PHILIPS 6 FT. 2-LAMP COLORTONE 50 DAYLIGHT
FLUORESCENT STRIP FIXTURE

STEEL FRAME LIGHTING ARMATURE

1 IN. CONTINUOUS STEEL ANGLE FOR
HAND SANDED ACRYLIC

1/4 IN. HAND SANDED ACRYLIC

1 IN. CONTINUOUS STEEL ANGLE
WELDED TO 1/8 IN. FLAT STEEL SPACER

1 IN. CUSTOM STEEL ANGLE "SHOE"

SECTION DETAIL CUSTOM LIGHT FIXTURE - EDGE

0 1   6   12 IN

ELECTRONIC DATA SYSTEMS CONTROL ROOM

Location: Plano, Texas

Architect: JPJ Architects

Lighting Designer: David A. Mintz, Inc., Lighting Consultants

Manufacturers: TIR (light tube, custom housing); GE (PAR lamps).

Date Completed: February 1990

Photography: Greg Hursley

In a state-of-the-art, NASA-like control room designed by JPJ Architects for Electronic Data Systems Corporation, a Texas-based company which manages one of the world's largest private digital networks, three critical factors influenced its innovative lighting scheme: the shape and size of the room, the tasks performed in it, and the fact that it operates 365 days a year, 24 hours a day. The lighting solution, devised by David A. Mintz, Inc., Lighting Consultants, combines two contradictory effects—diffuse yet highly directional illumination.

The arc-shaped control room was designed to accommodate more than 200 employees engaged in labor-intensive data processing and telecommunications management functions. The workers sit at computer workstations positioned along several rows of consoles and monitor images projected on large high-resolution screens. To prevent light reflections on the computer screens, the lighting designers avoided point sources. They also needed to keep workers positioned in one corner of the curved room from being distracted by light emanating from the ceiling in an opposite corner. Furthermore, the level of light reflecting from the surface of the front-projection screens is only about 8 footlamberts, so it was crucial to keep ambient light off the screens in order for the images to be clearly seen by the workers, some seated as far as 90 feet away. Finally, because operations take place constantly, the lighting needed to be maintained from above the ceiling to avoid interruption to the tasks being performed in the room.

To respond to all of these concerns, the lighting designers, working in tandem with the architects, created a cove lighting solution integrated within a coffered ceiling system, which allows light to bounce toward the back of the room without reflecting on the computer or large projection screens. The ceiling is composed of arced coffers to which coves of curved fabric-covered sound-absorbing panels are attached. To direct the light emanating from the coves toward the back of the room without bouncing back on the screens, the front of each of the coffers was painted white and the back painted black. To keep maintenance simple and at the same time evenly illuminate the coves, incandescent PAR lamps were used in conjunction with light pipes, which refract the light from a single source along the entire length of the pipe and provide about 5 footcandles of illumination on the worksurfaces below. Because the coves in the back of the room are shorter in length than those in front, light pipes six inches in diameter and varying in length were used with lamps ranging from 90 to 250 watts. The lamps are dimmed on different circuits to keep the light levels of higher-wattage lamps consistent with those of lower wattage.

The light pipe solution allowed all of the sources to be clustered along the radial spokes of the coffers. Custom fittings connected to the metal housings containing the lamps allow them to be lifted straight up with the flick of a lever so that they can be maintained from every other spoke, reducing the number of linear feet of catwalk required above the ceiling for access. Finally, the lighting designer suggested that finishes and furnishings be specified in dark colors with matte surfaces to keep reflection to a minimum.

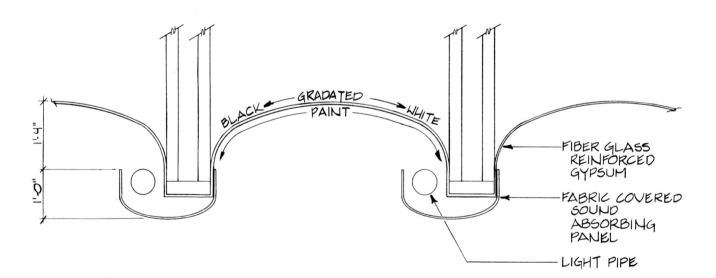

GIBSON DUNN & CRUTCHER

Location: New York, New York

Architect: Byrns, Kendall & Schieferdecker, Architects

Interior Designer: George Schieferdecker and Shannon McCarroll

Lighting Designer: Jerry Kugler Associates

Manufacturers: Ceiling fixture: Sylvania (fluorescent lamps); E.C.S. Mark Barchenko (fabricator brass plates, rods, fins, and milk white acrylic lenses). Wall Fixture: Sylvania (fluorescent lamps); E.C.S. Mark Barchenko (fabricator brass fins, steel rods, acrylic lens).

Date Completed: June 1989

Photography: Elliott Kaufman

Detail One: Ceiling Fixture

Although the former Pan Am Building, designed in 1963 by Emery Roth & Sons with Walter Gropius and Pietro Belluschi, is hardly an all-time favorite among those who appreciate architecture, architects Byrns, Kendall & Schieferdecker have nonetheless made remarkably elegant use of its elongated octagonal plan in the detailing of the offices they designed for the real estate law firm of Gibson Dunn & Crutcher. While the details reference the building's

shape, their relationship to the original structure ends there. Instead of the ponderous bulk that characterizes the building itself, the detailing possesses all the qualities that the building lacks: fine proportions, delicate refinement, and volumetric expression. The visual reference to the facade takes on various forms throughout the offices, and two of the most striking examples appear in custom light fixtures in the offices' elevator lobby and in a sculptural wall element screening the grand stairway.

Both fixtures are constructed of elegant materials that were used throughout the offices and express the building's shape in abstracted forms. The fixture suspended from the ceiling of the elevator lobby, a brass and acrylic rendition of the building's precast concrete elevation, sets the tone for the recurring visual theme and provides uplighting and diffuse downlighting for the lobby. Reflecting the facade's regular rhythm and periodic breaks, the fixture is divided into a series of six sections that run

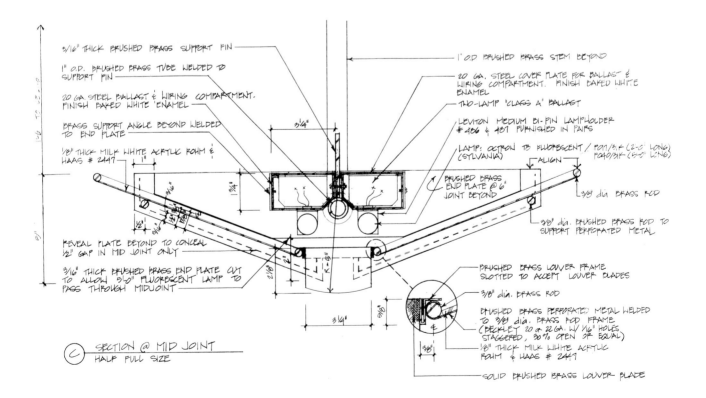

the length of the corridor and are divided by a central winged element composed of broad fabric-wrapped acoustical panels. (The perimeters of the corridor are fitted with continuous cove lighting to accentuate the elevators.)

Suspended from the ceiling by 1-inch-thick brushed brass tubes, each wing-shaped section of the fixture is composed of two angled, perforated brushed brass plates. The plates are welded to a brass rod frame adjoining a series of central brass fins, which serve as baffles spaced 1 inch on center. The

brass plates are topped by 1/8-inch-thick milk white acrylic to diffuse the light. Each section is capped by 3/16-inch-thick brushed brass end plates which are cut in the center to allow the fluorescent lamps to pass through the mid-joints. The fine detailing of the fixtures extends to the end plates, whose centerpoints are modulated with a keyhole motif.

The fixture is one of the earliest instances in which T-8 bi-pin fluorescent sources were chosen. About 25 percent more energy efficient than the old

T-12 lamps they replaced and providing almost the same light output, the triphosphor sources were also chosen for their color rendering capability. At 3,100 degrees Kelvin, their warmer light enhances the building materials used in this space—granite and travertine floors, African anigre wood paneling, and brass detailing. Their soft, diffuse, and fairly shadowless illumination is distributed upward to separate the fixture from the ceiling, and downward to illuminate the volume below.

Detail Two: Wall Fixture

In contrast to the lobby's ceiling fixture, the long linear fixture recessed into the sculptural wall facing the main stairwell is more simply detailed. Like the ceiling fixture, however, it is composed of brushed brass and acrylic and is characterized by fins.

Positioned vertically in an angled gray-green plaster wall, the fixture is the sole source of light for the tall, thin stairwell that joins one floor of the office to the other. Aesthetically, it also strongly reinforces the presence of the sculptural wall by accentuating its verticality and calling attention to its subtle color and texture.

Extending the full height of the wall, the 7½-inch-wide fixture is divided into two parts, separated by a square opening approximately three quarters of the way up the wall. Several pairs of the T-8 fluorescents are surface mounted within a 7½-inch-deep recess and faced by a 1/8-inch-thick milk white acrylic lens, which diffuses the light and precludes the need for staggering the lamps. The finlike louvers are positioned 2 inches on center in front of the lens and secured to a brushed brass frame fitted with rubber gasketing to prevent light leaks. The assembly is held in place by 1/4-inch-diameter brass rods threaded through the fins; by removing the rods it slips out for maintenance. In another nod to the building facade, the fixture's end plates, which are bolted to the opening in the sculptural wall, are loosely based on its octagonal shape.

Like the ceiling fixture, the sources in the wall fixture were chosen for their energy efficiency and for their ability to enhance the palette of the stairwell's materials, which include granite treads, mahogany risers, and brass stair rails. The lamp life of the sources is about 20,000 hours.

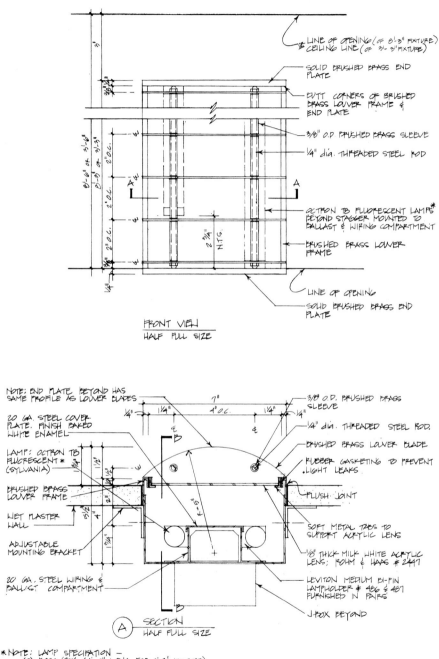

FRONT VIEW
HALF FULL SIZE

SECTION
HALF FULL SIZE

HIMMEL/BONNER ARCHITECTS

Location: Chicago, Illinois

Interior Designer: Himmel/Bonner Architects

Manufacturers: Metal Creations (structural rods, metal frame, baffles); Chicago Architectural Metals (brackets and poles); Janet Benes Studios (installation and translucent panels); Aiko Art Supply (parchment paper); Halo (MR-16 fixtures); GE (PAR 56 lamps).

Date Completed: March 1992

Photography: Marco Lorenzetti/Hedrich-Blessing

If Darcy Bonner's hobby of collecting rare and unusual insects seems to have little bearing on his professional practice as an architect, then one need look no further than a lighting fixture he designed for his firm's own offices to see that his avocation, in fact, has had considerable influence on the creativity that has driven his career. At first glance, it is difficult to imagine that the delicate, ethereal light fixture was actually inspired by a cumbersome, armor-clad Rhinoceros beetle, but a closer look at its constituent parts reveals the connections between one of nature's more unsightly creatures and Bonner's exquisite architectural correlative.

Located between the sliding wood double doors separating the office's reception area from the library/conference area behind it, the light fixture's structure is both a sculptural and functional centerpiece in the dividing line between these two spaces. Based on the spindly segments of the beetle's legs, the structure is defined by two polished steel poles that are set 18 inches apart and extend from floor to ceiling. Set in a slip connection bolted to the floor, the lower portions of the poles are 30-inch-

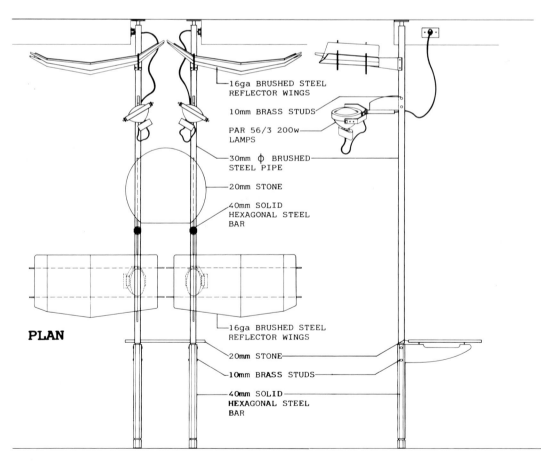

16ga BRUSHED STEEL REFLECTOR WINGS

10mm BRASS STUDS

PAR 56/3 200w LAMPS

30mm φ BRUSHED STEEL PIPE

20mm STONE

40mm SOLID HEXAGONAL STEEL BAR

16ga BRUSHED STEEL REFLECTOR WINGS

20mm STONE

10mm BRASS STUDS

40mm SOLID HEXAGONAL STEEL BAR

PLAN

FRONT VIEW   **SIDE VIEW**

long hexagonal steel rods. Welded to these rods are 66-inch-long rounded tubes that are fitted to another slip connection in the ceiling.

Three sets of armlike fins extend from the two poles to support the functional elements of the light fixture. Two 12-inch-long painted aluminum fins—attached to the poles with brass dowels at the point where the hexagonal and rounded sections of the poles meet—support Bonner's abstracted yet functional impression of the beetle's body: a 3/4-inch-thick slab shelf of marble that is 20 inches in diameter. Similar 16-inch-long fins of brushed steel are bracketed to the upper portions of the poles and support 3-foot-long-by-15-inch-wide reflecting plates, which are cantilevered 7 inches beneath the ceiling. Also made of brushed steel, the plates are ribbed and bent, like the armored plates of the beetle's shell. Another set of painted aluminum fins connected to the upper portions of the poles support two large 200-watt PAR 56 lamps located 12 inches beneath the brushed steel plates. The powerful light of the PAR 56 lamps, which are connected to the electrical system running through a dropped ceiling grid, reflects off the extended steel plates above them back to the floor to provide the ambient light for the reception area.

In pursuing his entomological fascination, Bonner discovered a mystery that inspired another dramatic element that extends his poetic interpretation of the lowly bug beyond the bounds of the central light fixture into the library/conference room. The beetles' gossamer cellophane wings have been translated into membranes of parchment paper stretched like a kite over two delicately curving metal frames that sweep from one end of the library/conference room's ceiling to the other. Suspended by hidden hooks, the vast winglike membranes cover long tubular 40-watt incandescent lamps in mounted to the acoustical ceiling, allowing the room to be washed in warm diffused light that complements the furnishings.

Running down the spine between the two wings and complementing the warm diffuse glow are MR-16 track lights separated by black custom-designed baffles. Along the axis of this lighted spine, a sandblasted glass panel, cut to fill the 18-inch-wide gap between the poles of the sculptural light fixture in the doorway, metaphorically connects the diaphanous wings to the primary fixture. The floor-to-ceiling panel is placed two feet behind the poles, however, defining the outer boundary of the library/conference room, while loosely integrating the disparate elements of the overall lighting plan in these two rooms. It is the final touch in a scheme that brings the splendors Bonner finds in a gigantic creeping bug infinitely broader appeal.

ISLAND TRADING COMPANY

Location: New York, New York

Interior Designer: Kevin Walz Design

Lighting Designer: Kevin Walz

Manufacturers: Uplight sconces: GE (PAR 38 quartz lamps); Renaissance Workshop (aluminum reflectors). General downlight and wall washers: GE (PAR 38 quartz lamps); Stonco (socket); Renaissance Workshop (aluminum baffle, galvanized steel stem, solid brass bar stock). Reception pendant: Renaissance Workshop (galvanized steel stem); Ain Plastic (bronze-mirrored disk).

Date Completed: October 1991

Photography: Eduard Hueber/Arch Photo

Detail One: Family of Fixtures

The Island Trading Company, a division of Island Records, is located on the top floor of an industrial building off Broadway in Manhattan. For its offices, designer Kevin Walz used simple, inexpensive materials in untraditional ways to create a sophisticated, yet down-to-earth space. Two themes dominated his approach to the offices' space plan:

Island Trading Company's product—music—and its democratic style of doing business. Walz's innovative approach to cultivating a relaxed, visual rhythm in the space extends to every detail—from the villagelike plan with traffic areas along windowed walls to the natural materials used throughout. To keep down costs, he used standard light fixtures with custom-designed shades

and reflectors, taking care to integrate them with the surroundings.

Three of the most notable of these fixtures appear in or near the conference room, while a fourth is in the reception area. Though each of the three conference-room fixtures has a different purpose, they work together—supplemented by daylight streaming in through an overhead skylight—to complete the

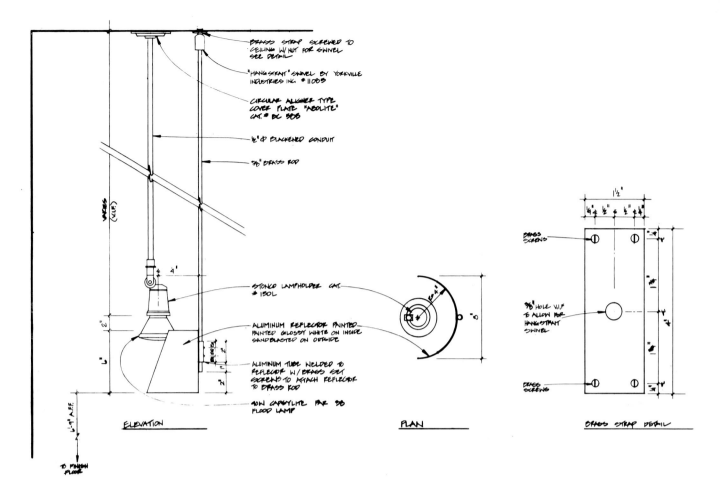

BRASS STRAP SCREWED TO
CEILING W/ NUT FOR SWIVEL
SEE DETAIL

"HANG STRAP" SWIVEL BY YORKVILLE
INDUSTRIES INC. # 11005

CIRCULAR ALIGNER TYPE
COVER PLATE "NEOLITE"
CAT.# BC 505

½"⌀ BLACKENED CONDUIT

⅜" BRASS ROD

VARIES
(V.I.F.)

4'

STONKO LAMPHOLDER CAT.
150L

2"

ALUMINUM REFLECTOR PAINTED
PAINTED GLOSSY WHITE ON INSIDE
SANDBLASTED ON OUTSIDE

6"

ALUMINUM TUBE WELDED TO
REFLECTOR W/ BRASS SET
SCREWS TO ATTACH REFLECTOR
TO BRASS ROD

2"

40W CAPSYLITE PAR 38
FLOOD LAMP

8'-9" A.F.F.

TO FINISH
FLOOR

ELEVATION

PLAN

BRASS STRAP DETAIL

1½"

¼" ½" ½" ¼"

BRASS
SCREWS

⅜" HOLE V.I.F.
TO ALLOW FOR
HANG STRAP
SWIVEL

BRASS
SCREWS

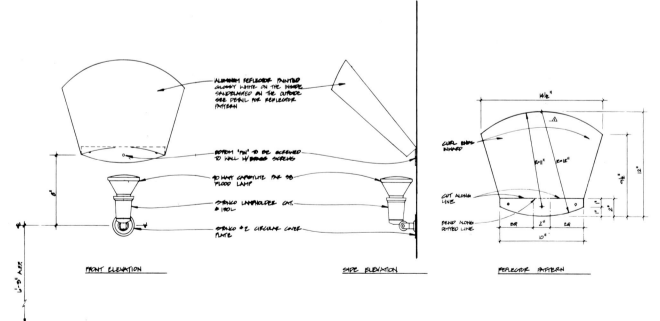

ALUMINUM REFLECTOR PAINTED
GLOSSY WHITE ON THE INSIDE
SANDBLASTED ON THE OUTSIDE
SEE DETAIL FOR REFLECTOR
PATTERN

BOTTOM "FIN" TO BE SCREWED
TO WALL W/ BRASS SCREWS

40 WATT CAPSYLITE PAR 38
FLOOD LAMP

STONKO LAMPHOLDER CAT.
150L

STONKO #2 CIRCULAR COVER
PLATE

6"

4'-0" A.F.F.

TO FINISH FLOOR

FRONT ELEVATION

SIDE ELEVATION

REFLECTOR PATTERN

14½"

CURL ENDS
INWARD

R=11" R=12"

12"

CUT ALONG
LINE

BEND ALONG
DOTTED LINE

EQ 2" EQ

2"

10"

JACK MORTON PRODUCTIONS

Location: San Francisco, California

Architect: Interior Architects

Lighting Designer: Lighting Integration Technology

Manufacturers: General Electric (MR-16s); Lutron (dimming system); Translite Systems (wall and lamp brackets, cables).

Date Completed: October 1992

Photography: Beatriz Coll

The offices of Jack Morton Productions, a video production studio designed by Interior Architects, are located on the top floor of a high-ceilinged loft building in San Francisco. The design of these offices allows for uninterrupted views to the outside from the open office spaces in the core of the 9,000-square-foot space through the partially walled perimeter offices. IA's designer, Tony Garrett, with the assistance of lighting designer Susan Huey of Lighting Integration Technology, devised a minimalist lighting system in the perimeter offices that meets the functional task lighting requirements without interfering with the views, and responds to the demands of a limited budget.

Complementing the spare interior design, the lighting system consists simply of off-the-shelf, 50-watt MR-16 fixtures suspended by custom brackets on two cables that stretch from one interior wall to the other. Located above the worksurfaces in each perimeter office, the low-voltage fixtures suspended from the V-shaped steel rods are fully adjustable, as are the brackets themselves. The brackets may be moved vertically or horizontally along the cables, and once adjusted as desired, are locked onto the cables with a custom screw mechanism. The 1/8-inch-diameter, 14-foot-long aluminum cables are supported by polished chrome brackets bolted to each wall and positioned 9 feet above

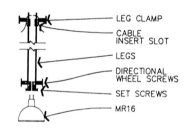

LEG CLAMP
CABLE INSERT SLOT
LEGS
DIRECTIONAL WHEEL SCREWS
SET SCREWS
MR16

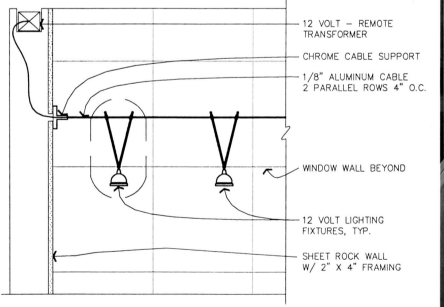

12 VOLT – REMOTE TRANSFORMER
CHROME CABLE SUPPORT
1/8" ALUMINUM CABLE 2 PARALLEL ROWS 4" O.C.
WINDOW WALL BEYOND
12 VOLT LIGHTING FIXTURES, TYP.
SHEET ROCK WALL W/ 2" X 4" FRAMING

the floor—well above the head of the average occupant yet easily accessible when adjustments are necessary. Since the project was budget driven, the lamps—at approximately $40 a piece—were selected for their low cost. But, in keeping with the minimalist aesthetic sought by the designer, their small size was also a factor in their specification.

Each office has its own transformer, discretely positioned in a U-channel in the top of the interior wall. The transformers are not only easily accessible, but their close proximity to the fixtures significantly prevents voltage drop. Individual switches with a manual dimming system also allow the low-voltage fixtures to be controlled separately. Each transformer is equipped with an integral circuit breaker, which automatically shuts down the electrical system to prevent an electrical short.

The minimalist lighting system in the perimeter offices is part of an overall layered lighting strategy: Daylight through the windows; fluorescent lighting in the open office areas for contrasting color quality and higher light output; and task lighting on the worksurfaces.

LOVINGER COHN & ASSOCIATES

Location: New York, New York

Architect: V. Polsinelli Architects

Lighting Designer: Lynn Redding

Manufacturers: Lightolier (PAR 38 track fixture); Edison Price (downlight fixtures); Artimede (surface-mounted fixtures); Flos (outrigger fixtures).

Date Completed: November 1992

Photography: Paul Warchol

Detail One: Recessed Ceiling Feature

In converting an 1871 structure in lower Manhattan into offices for Lovinger Cohn & Associates, a television and film production company, architect Vincent Polsinelli made the most of the offices's tight interior spaces with a skillful use of materials and light. Formerly occupied by a butter and cheese warehouse, the two-story building has a long, narrow confining footprint whose only exposure to natural light is from its north-facing facade. While the architect's orientation of the plan and his use of glass walls, glass-block floors and ceilings, and a skylight allow natural light to penetrate deep into the interior spaces, his innovative artificial lighting solutions, developed in conjuction with lighting designer Lynn Redding, create an added sense of expansiveness.

The production offices and the conference room particularly reveal the artful coupling of natural and artificial light. In the production offices on the second floor, two lighting features work together to open up the space: a skylight atop a domed cupola and track lights recessed within a pair of ceiling coves. The cupola was uncovered during demolition, and the architect took advantage of the possibility of lighting the space vertically by capping it with a skylight. To further extend the space, both vertically and laterally, he broke the ceiling plane where it intersects with the walls on two sides by introducing 1-foot-wide recesses along the length of the room. The coves are fitted with track fixtures and covered with laminated glass diffusers to wash the walls with evenly distributed light and make the width of the space appear larger. Because the diffusers are positioned above the ceiling plane, the lighted coves also lift the space upward at its edges. A groove on one side holds the diffuser in place, which simply tilts out for access to the lamps.

The 5-foot design module dictated the width of the coves, which occupy 1 foot on either side of the 22-foot-wide space. The 2-foot-deep recess contains 17 150-watt PAR 38 flood lamps postioned 18 inches on center and aimed at the wall. The milky white diffuser, placed 8 inches above the ceiling plane, allows the light to appear as a continuous band of light.

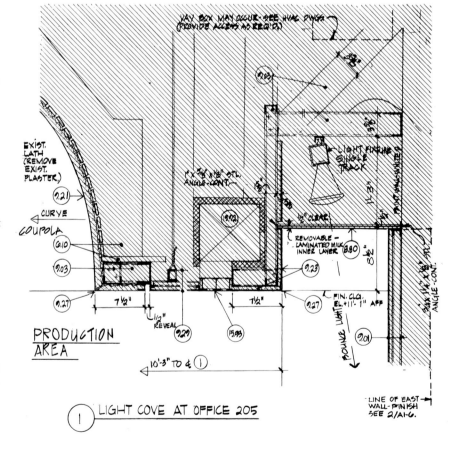

LIGHT COVE AT OFFICE 205

Lovinger Cohn & Associates

Detail Two: Conference Room Light Box

Lovinger Cohn's conference room was designed to be a glowing light box in and of itself. The double-height space is topped with a glass-block ceiling, which serves as the floor to the outdoor terrace above, and appears to extend the room even higher. Located in the back of the building, the glass ceiling allows sunlight into the space during the day and is illuminated at night by direct and reflected light coming from adjoining spaces above.

The incandescent light from ceiling-recessed wall washers in a seating area next to the terrace bounces off the far wall, through glass walls on the opposite side, and spills onto the glass terrace floor into the conference room below. Supplementing the warm light of the eight 100-watt A 19 sources, whose light is directed evenly toward the white-painted wall, is light from five 100-watt A lamps surface-mounted to a parapet wall above the terrace and covered with decorative sanded glass diffusers, which evenly spread the light. It was critical to illuminate the glass ceiling from above at night, so that it wouldn't become blackened as glass surfaces do when the sky goes dark. The light from the incandescent sources sufficiently illuminates the conference room in the evening with ambient light from above, while two other custom fixtures provide task illumination over the conference table both day and night.

The task sources are 30-foot-long "outriggers" which extend from the 7½-foot-high mezzanine level into the space. Each is composed of a black-painted steel U channel facing down, and connected to a yoke flange bolted to the I-beam supporting the mezzanine floor. The channels are further supported by stainless-steel cables extending from its center and fastened to the I-beam. Each outrigger contains two 50-watt low-voltage MR-16s connected to clip plates attached to the U channels. Providing a concentrated highlight on the conference table, the MR-16s can be moved by sliding the clip plates along the channel. Wiring extends from the transformer/junction box behind the I-beam through the channel.

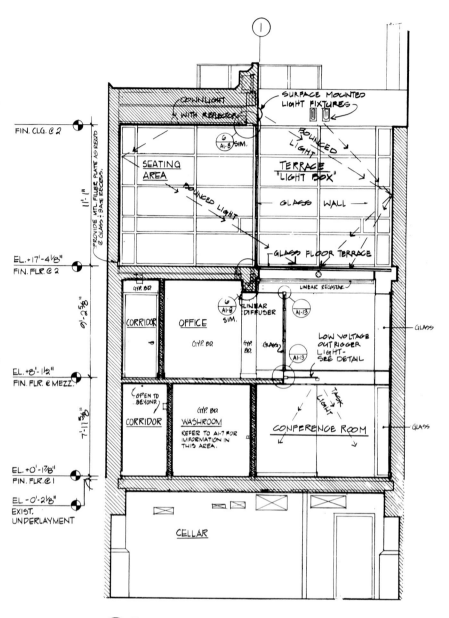

BUILDING SECTION

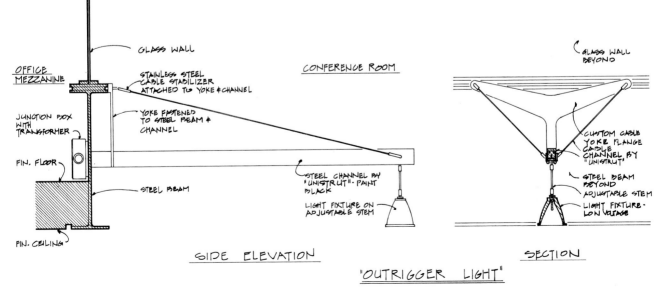

OFFICE
MEZZANINE

GLASS WALL

STAINLESS STEEL
CABLE STABILIZER
ATTACHED TO YOKE & CHANNEL

CONFERENCE ROOM

JUNCTION BOX
WITH
TRANSFORMER

YOKE FASTENED
TO STEEL BEAM &
CHANNEL

FIN. FLOOR

STEEL BEAM

STEEL CHANNEL BY
"UNISTRUT"- PAINT
BLACK

LIGHT FIXTURE ON
ADJUSTABLE STEM

FIN. CEILING

GLASS WALL
BEYOND

CUSTOM CABLE
YOKE FLANGE
CABLE
CHANNEL BY
"UNISTRUT"

STEEL BEAM
BEYOND
ADJUSTABLE STEM

LIGHT FIXTURE -
LOW VOLTAGE

SIDE ELEVATION

SECTION

"OUTRIGGER LIGHT"

NATIONAL AUDUBON SOCIETY HEADQUARTERS

Location: New York, New York

Architect: Croxton Collaborative

Lighting Designer: Flack+Kurtz

Manufacturer: T.I.R. (light pipe).

Date Completed: October 1993

Photography: Jeff Goldberg/ESTO

The widely published Manhattan headquarters for the National Audubon Society, designed by the Croxton Collaborative, has been lauded for its sophisticated environmental planning and energy efficiency. From its recycling chutes to its gas-fired heating and cooling system to its minimal use of toxic substances in furnishings and materials, the headquarters is a composite of layered strategies which together create an energy-efficient, clean building. While the lighting throughout the space has also been designed to reduce energy consumption, one lighting element stands out for its

aesthetic integration as well as its energy efficiency. Located on the top floor of the 8-story building, the lighting feature integrates the effects of an off-the-shelf internal reflectance light tube with natural daylight coming through a peaked skylight above the roof.

In developing the lighting solution for this area of the Audubon headquarters, lighting designers Flack+Kurtz chose the light tube to meet the demands of three basic criteria: they needed a low-wattage source that would be easy to maintain and could provide both up- and downlight. The clear acrylic light tube that was selected is similar in concept to fiber-optic lighting in that a single source illuminates the entire tube. The tube is lined with a prismatic film that redirects the light from a 250-watt metal halide down the length of the tube. Fluorescent sources were also considered as an alternative to

the light tube since they are more energy efficient, but they were ruled out because their light output level was higher than the architects desired—the fluorescents provide 750 lumens/foot vs. the 175 lumens/foot of the metal halides used in conjunction with the light tube. In addition, the tube is easier to maintain and can be relamped without the use of scaffolding, since the tube and not the lamp is positioned over the open stair.

Beneath the peaked vertical shaft of the skylight, two 37-foot-long light tubes were positioned in niches designed to receive them so that they serve visually as a precursor to the skylight without protruding into the space. They emit light up toward the face of the vertical walls of the shaft supporting the skylight, giving the walls a luminous finish and allowing light to spill into the skylight at night. They also emit light downward to pro-

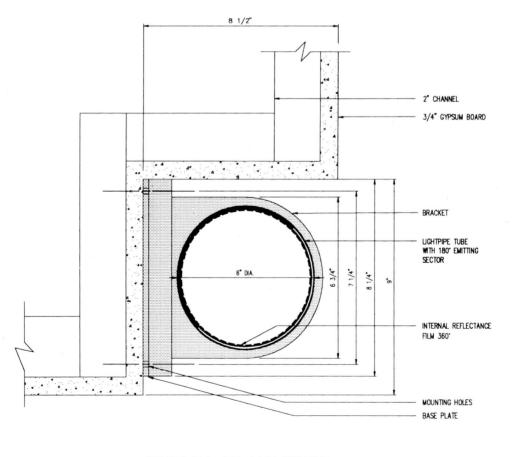

SECTION AT LIGHTPIPE

vide sufficient light on cloudy days. Because the lighting designers wanted the light to be directed up toward the walls at a 45-degree angle, the prismatic film within the light tube was cut to create a light emitting sector of 180 degrees, which was angled for direction toward the specific surfaces. The white vertical surfaces also have a high reflectance value so that the light sources become more energy efficient. To meet the architects'

specification for a warmer light in the space, the metal halides lamps were color-corrected to a temperature of about 3,200 degrees Kelvin.

The up- and downlight effects of the light tube were balanced with the other two criteria of low-wattage and easy maintenance. Complying with the New York State Energy Conservation Code, which allows 2.4 watts/square foot, the two metal halides and the ballasts gener-

ate a total of 560 watts, for an average lighting load of less than 1 watt/square foot. Additionally, the two sources are surface-mounted at one end of the shaft and are left exposed for ease of maintenance. The sources are also connected to an astronomical time clock, which turns the lights on and off at different times throughout the course of the year. The lamp life of these sources is about 10,000 hours.

PLAYBOY

Location: New York, New York

Architect: Himmel Bonner Architects

Lighting Designer: Flack+Kurtz

Manufacturers: Rambusch (quartz fixtures); Melto Metalworks (reflector, arms, housing).

Date Completed: May 1993

Photography: Scott Frances/ESTO

Within the rich, historical context of the landmarked 1920s Crown Building on 57th Street in Manhattan, Himmel Bonner Architects have designed classic contemporary offices for Playboy Enterprises with unique materials and inventive finishes in a style that is likely to stand the test of time as gracefully as the building itself. A central, double-height atrium is the heart of the plan, and the openness it establishes expands through the transparent and translucent walls surrounding it to the open and private offices ringing its perimeter. All of the interior spaces are distinguished as much by interesting architectural forms and a rich palette of materials, colors, and textures as they are by the architects' imaginative attention to details.

The cleverly developed detailing extends to the lighting, perhaps the most unique expression of which appears in the form of custom-designed, attennaelike fixtures mounted to the railing of a glass wall surrounding the atrium on the second floor. The atrium is a study in contrasts—of coolness and warmth, of light and dark—with the warm leather-tiled treads of its staircase set against the cool glass walls around its perimeter, and the light, creamy expanses of its French limestone floor and textured ceiling sandwiching slivers of darkness—which include platinum gray-painted steel mullions and stair rails as well as the attennaelike fixtures themselves. Not only do the unusual forms of these fixtures enliven the atrium's streamlined, open expanse with integrated and dynamic points of punctuation, but the quality and intensity of the light from the sources they house bathe the atrium in a bright, white light that distinguishes it from the other

spaces in the office.

Conceived of by the architects and developed in conjunction with lighting designers Flack+Kurtz, the ten double-headed fixtures surrounding the atrium were designed to uplight the ceiling, highlighting its deep texture and indirectly bouncing light back into the space. Each fixture consists of a shovel-like, black-painted aluminum head containing an asymmetric reflector and a 300-watt quartz lamp. The shovel-like assembly is supported by a 1/2-inch-diameter rigid, bent-steel rod, which is attached at one end to a yoke connected to the fixture head and at the other to a steel plate mounted to the mullions

between the glass wall surrounding the perimeter of the atrium.

Particular care was given to the positioning of the fixtures. They were designed to rise well above eye-level to avoid glare, yet be far enough away from the ceiling to allow for a fair distribution of light on its textured surface. They also extend into the atrium so that their light, which the reflectors throw in one direction, would be focused primarily in the center of the ceiling.

At 2,900 degrees Kelvin, the quartz sources were chosen for their bright, white light, which was intended to create a sense of being outdoors. The idea was to create a qualitative contrast

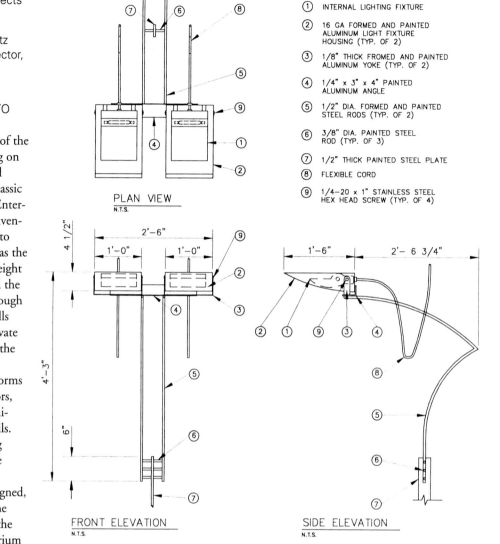

NOTES

1. INTERNAL LIGHTING FIXTURE
2. 16 GA FORMED AND PAINTED ALUMINUM LIGHT FIXTURE HOUSING (TYP. OF 2)
3. 1/8" THICK FROMED AND PAINTED ALUMINUM YOKE (TYP. OF 2)
4. 1/4" x 3" x 4" PAINTED ALUMINUM ANGLE
5. 1/2" DIA. FORMED AND PAINTED STEEL RODS (TYP. OF 2)
6. 3/8" DIA. PAINTED STEEL ROD (TYP. OF 3)
7. 1/2" THICK PAINTED STEEL PLATE
8. FLEXIBLE CORD
9. 1/4–20 x 1" STAINLESS STEEL HEX HEAD SCREW (TYP. OF 4)

PLAN VIEW
N.T.S.

FRONT ELEVATION
N.T.S.

SIDE ELEVATION
N.T.S.

between the light in the atrium and the warmer light of the PAR 20 mono-points in the circulation areas as well as the cooler light of the fluorescents in the open-office areas. A brightness level of 25 footcandles produced by the ten double-headed fixtures also distinguishes the atrium from the lower levels in the circulation areas and the higher levels in the perimeter task areas. The fixtures are powered by cords which extend to a junction box contained within the ceiling beams and echo the slender lines of the supporting steel rods.

REGENT COURT

Location: Dearborn, Michigan

Architect: Neumann Smith & Associates

Lighting Designer: Illuminart, Stefan Graf

Landscape Designer: Grissim Metz Associates

Manufacturers: Wall Pockets: Engineered Lighting Products. Ceiling Cove: Linear Lighting, Legion (fixtures); Osram/Sylvania (lamps). Metal Halide Systems: Spaulding, Elliptipar, Power-lite (fixtures); GE, Osram/Sylvania, and Venture (lamps). Exterior bollards: Dan Daily Manufacturing (custom bollard housing); Hadco, Stonco, Moldcast (luminaires); GE, Osram/Sylvania, Venture (lamps). Landscape lighting: Greenlee, Kim, Power-lite, Hydrel, Devine.

Date Completed: September 1990

Photography: Gary Quesada/Balthazar Korab

Detail One: Wall Pockets

In developing the lighting concept for the entrance atrium of the Regent Court office building in Dearborn Michigan, lighting designer Stefan Graf of Illuminart worked with architects Neumann Smith & Associates in the schematic phase of the design process. Graf suggested an understated, integrated solution that would allow the lines and planes of the architecture to stand out by minimizing the presence of the light sources. Three sources in particular work together to provide the overall illumination in the atrium, and because two of them are indirect and reflect off the architectural surfaces, the architecture, in effect, becomes a luminous reflector of light.

The two indirect sources complement one another to light the undulating walkways on every floor surrounding the central atrium without penetrating the ceiling planes above with downlights. By freeing the ceiling planes from direct downlight, not only is the architecture unobstructed, but it can be viewed from the ground level without glare. One indirect lighting feature playing a role in this liminal lighting solution is a series of pocket lights embedded in the balcony rails around each of the ten floors of the building. The other is a continuous 4-inch-wide ceiling cove with a matte white diffuser above the elevators.

The lighting designer requested that provisions be made in the balcony rails to accommodate the pocket lights, so that a pathway illumination level of 3 to 6 footcandles and uniformity ratios of 5 to 1 would be maintained. Designed to be 6 inches deep, the rail contains a pocket that accommodates a 13-watt compact fluorescent lamp and an asymmetric specular reflector that indirectly projects the light onto the walkway. The aperture through which the light emanates is 6 inches wide by 10 inches high and is positioned 2 feet above the floor. Though the walkway's carpeting needed to be dark enough to be easily maintained, the lighting designer requested that it, along with the vertical surfaces in the spaces, be as light in color as possible to maintain a high reflectance value.

The 13-watt compact fluorescent lamps with built-in ballasts were selected for their efficiency, size, brightness (900 lumens/lamp), and good color rendering. They also have a color temperature of 3,500 degrees Kelvin—which needed to match the color of the fluorescent sources in the cove above the elevators while offering a warmer light in the interior public areas. They were used in downlights in other corridors as well, thereby allowing a significant portion of the overall light sources in the building to be standardized. The lighting designer also specified a clear Plexiglas lamp guard to keep dust and debris from entering the light pocket, as well as to protect the lamp from being touched by anyone inadvertently reaching in.

Regent Court

Detail Two: Ceiling Cove

Like the pocket lights in the balcony rail, the ceiling cove fixtures above the elevators in Regent Court also utilize an indirect system. The cove not only keeps the ceiling plane free of apertures, but offers a focal glow upon the elevators, which are key destinations along the walkways. A linear T-8 fluorescent source was used to enhance the lines of the architecture by reflecting off the walls to help illuminate the sinuous walkway.

A semi-specular continuous parabolic reflector system helps distribute the light from above the elevators out into the lobby walkway. The lamp is concealed by a reflector baffle, which also eliminates direct glare in the high-traffic area. Since it is reflected away from the wall, the light from the cove is well distributed.

All of the sources were chosen for their long-term energy efficiency. Early participation by the lighting designer in the design process also aided in reducing construction and maintenance costs. Electronic ballasts (more efficient than magnetic ballasts) were specified, and overall illumination levels vary from 6 to 30 footcandles. All lamps have a rated life of 10,000 hours or greater, all luminaires are easily accessible for maintenance, and the average lighting load is a very low .7 watts per square foot. An astronomical time clock controls the light and is programmed to illuminate various areas as needed throughout the course of the day and night.

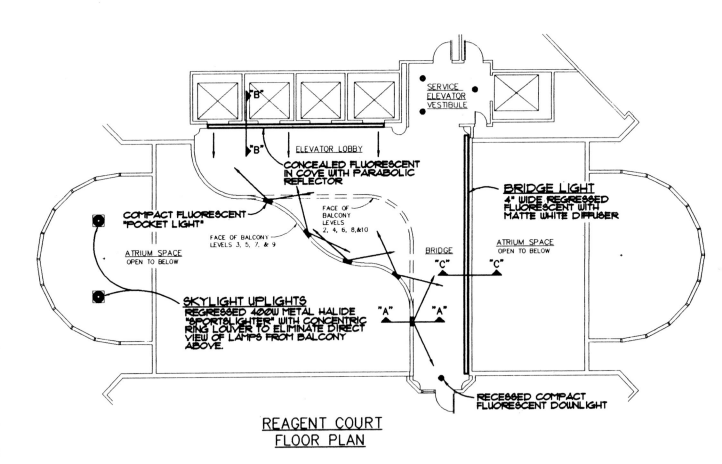

REAGENT COURT
FLOOR PLAN

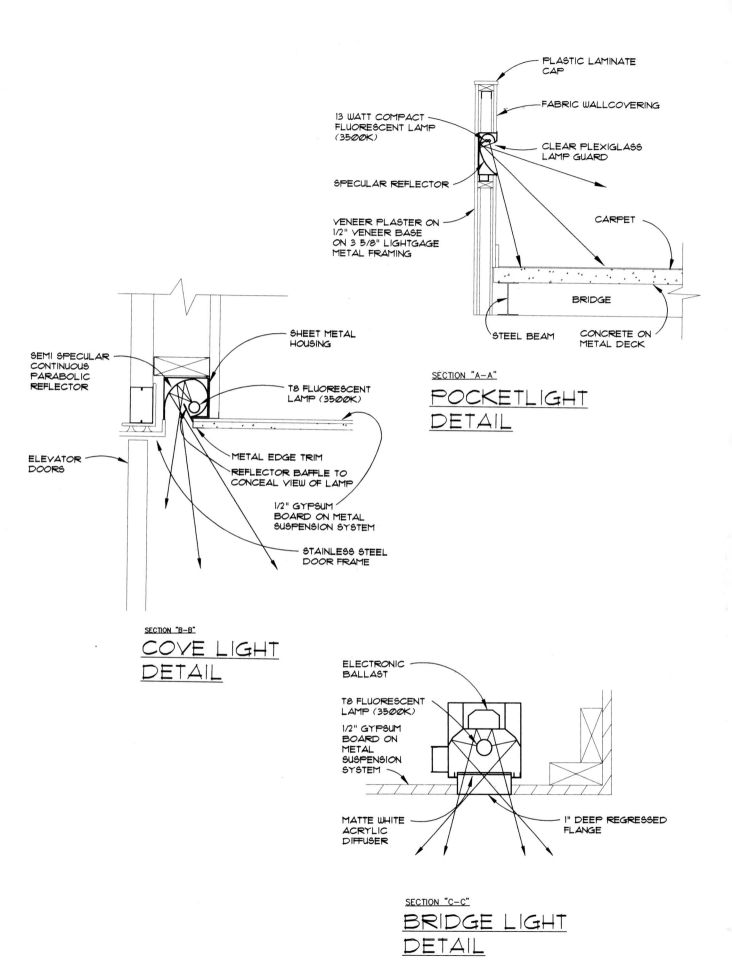

PLASTIC LAMINATE
CAP

FABRIC WALLCOVERING

13 WATT COMPACT
FLUORESCENT LAMP
(3500K)

CLEAR PLEXIGLASS
LAMP GUARD

SPECULAR REFLECTOR

CARPET

VENEER PLASTER ON
1/2" VENEER BASE
ON 3 5/8" LIGHTGAGE
METAL FRAMING

BRIDGE

STEEL BEAM

CONCRETE ON
METAL DECK

SECTION "A-A"

POCKETLIGHT DETAIL

SEMI SPECULAR
CONTINUOUS
PARABOLIC
REFLECTOR

SHEET METAL
HOUSING

T8 FLUORESCENT
LAMP (3500K)

ELEVATOR
DOORS

METAL EDGE TRIM

REFLECTOR BAFFLE TO
CONCEAL VIEW OF LAMP

1/2" GYPSUM
BOARD ON METAL
SUSPENSION SYSTEM

STAINLESS STEEL
DOOR FRAME

SECTION "B-B"

COVE LIGHT DETAIL

ELECTRONIC
BALLAST

T8 FLUORESCENT
LAMP (3500K)

1/2" GYPSUM
BOARD ON
METAL
SUSPENSION
SYSTEM

MATTE WHITE
ACRYLIC
DIFFUSER

1" DEEP REGRESSED
FLANGE

SECTION "C-C"

BRIDGE LIGHT DETAIL

Regent Court

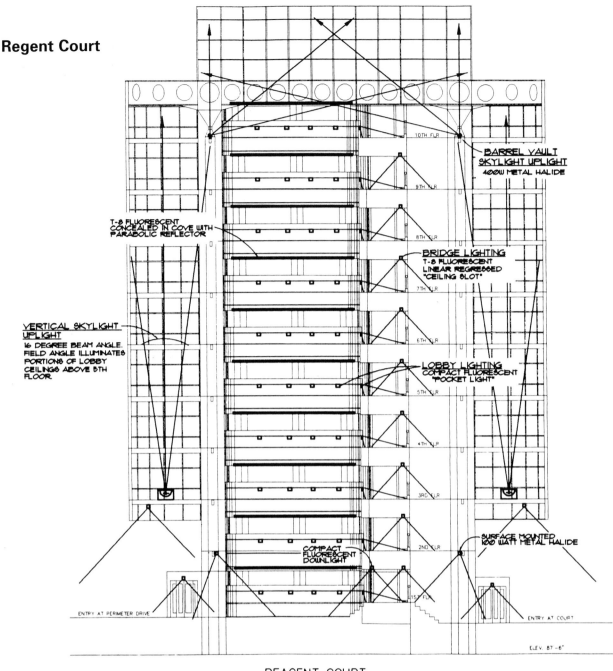

Regent Court

BARREL VAULT
SKYLIGHT UPLIGHT
400W METAL HALIDE

T-8 FLUORESCENT
CONCEALED IN COVE WITH
PARABOLIC REFLECTOR

BRIDGE LIGHTING
T-8 FLUORESCENT
LINEAR REGRESSED
"CEILING SLOT"

VERTICAL SKYLIGHT
UPLIGHT
16 DEGREE BEAM ANGLE.
FIELD ANGLE ILLUMINATES
PORTIONS OF LOBBY
CEILINGS ABOVE 5TH
FLOOR

LOBBY LIGHTING
COMPACT FLUORESCENT
"POCKET LIGHT"

COMPACT
FLUORESCENT
DOWNLIGHT

SURFACE MOUNTED
100 WATT METAL HALIDE

ENTRY AT PERIMETER DRIVE

ENTRY AT COURT

ELEV. 87'-6"

10TH FLR / 9TH FLR / 8TH FLR / 7TH FLR / 6TH FLR / 5TH FLR / 4TH FLR / 3RD FLR / 2ND FLR / 1ST FLR

REAGENT COURT
BUILDING SECTION

Detail Three: Perimeter Uplights

While the two indirect sources enhance the walls and ceilings of the architecture in Regent Court's atrium interior, the third significant lighting feature illuminates the glass-enclosed perimeter walls of the three barrel-vaulted forms, two of which rise vertically above the atrium's front and rear entrance to the top of the building, and the third caps the building and serves as an overhead skylight. The lighting objectives are two-fold: to establish the building as a landmark after dark, calling attention to its scale and height by highlighting its frame-

work and mullions; and to increase the perception of brightness in the atrium.

The sources that accomplish these objectives are eight 400-watt metal halide uplights. Four are positioned as uplights, concealed in pairs at the base of each of the vertical vaults. Typically used in sports stadiums, the 22-inch-diameter luminaires are recessed in 2½-foot-deep cavities in the floor and project light up through vaults, highlighting their white-painted mullions and reflecting off the ceiling above. The other four metal halides, equipped with metal reflectors, are positioned on cross

beams above the atrium and project light across the horizontal skylight atop the structure. Since there is no public access to the floors of the vertical glass vaults, direct viewing into the uplights is not a central issue. However, a concentric ringed louver visor minimizes source illuminance when occupants look down from the balcony. The reflector is also covered with a glass lens to keep out dust and dirt, and an access panel was created for the remote ballast.

To provide continuous illumination along the vaults, the angle of the beam spreads of these sources was carefully

Regent Court

considered. The optics of the reflector control the beam spread to a tight 16-degree angle so that most of the light penetrates directly through the height of the shaft. The sources that light the tops of the vaults are positioned so that their beam candlepower is directed toward the center of the horizontal vault. The uplights provide illumination to portions of the lobby ceilings above the fifth floor. Though their primary purpose is to light the vaults, the metal halides contribute a total of 120,000 lumens to the atrium and enhance the ambient lighting in the lobby, causing it to appear brighter.

The color of the 4,100-degree Kelvin lamps offers a cooler white light that contrasts with the warmer 3,500-degree Kelvin fluorescents in the lobby, heightening the sense of warmth light in the public areas. The metal halides are controlled by an astronomical time clock that turns them on only after dark. Their lamp life is rated at 20,000 hours.

Detail Four: Exterior Bollards

Regent Court's exterior lighting concept makes the building visible from the street at night. Outside, a series of custom-designed, pylon-shaped bollards cast animated light upon a landscaped motorcourt, whereas by day they stand as sleek sculptural forms against the linear character of the building. Interspersed throughout the landscape, the five bollards differ in height from 12 to 20 feet to artistically accommodate the aiming angles required of the lamps housed within them. Surrounded by the wings of the building flanking the central vault above the entrance atrium, the landscape is also composed of sculptural rolling ribbons, alternately topped with grass or brick pavers with sidewalls of black granite.

A rectangular enclosure complementing the contemporary geometry of the architecture, each bollard is constructed of black-painted aluminum and contains 240-watt PAR 56 and 75-watt PAR 36 12-volt lamps with remote transformers at the base. The lamps are covered with louvers specifically manu-

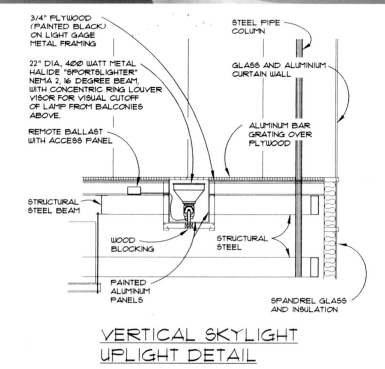

3/4" PLYWOOD (PAINTED BLACK) ON LIGHT GAGE METAL FRAMING

22" DIA., 400 WATT METAL HALIDE "SPORTSLIGHTER" NEMA 2, 16 DEGREE BEAM, WITH CONCENTRIC RING LOUVER VISOR FOR VISUAL CUTOFF OF LAMP FROM BALCONIES ABOVE.

REMOTE BALLAST WITH ACCESS PANEL

STEEL PIPE COLUMN

GLASS AND ALUMINIUM CURTAIN WALL

ALUMINUM BAR GRATING OVER PLYWOOD

STRUCTURAL STEEL BEAM

WOOD BLOCKING

STRUCTURAL STEEL

PAINTED ALUMINUM PANELS

SPANDREL GLASS AND INSULATION

VERTICAL SKYLIGHT UPLIGHT DETAIL

factured to adjust to different aiming angles. The angles of the blades vary from 32 to 48 degrees to shield glare. And the covers are demountable for access to the lamps and ballasts.

To heighten the dynamics of the illuminated sculptural elements, the lamps are connected to a four-circuit, electronically-timed crossfader, which is set to fade every 7 seconds and slowly change the lighted patterns on the landscape. The incandescent sources are also dimmed 10 percent to extend their lamp life.

Complementing the light from the bollards are 100-watt metal halide uplights positioned around the perimeter of the motorcourt. At 3,000 degrees Kelvin, they articulate the architecture surrounding the court, while cooler 4,100-degree Kelvin metal halides uplight the trees. All of the court lighting is controlled by an astronomical time clock for ease of operation.

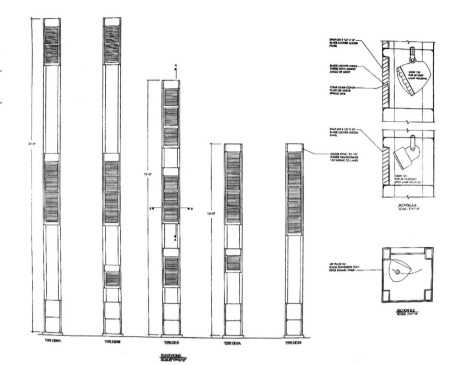

TOMMY BOY MUSIC

Location: New York, New York
Interior Architect: Turett Collaborative
Lighting Designer: Gary Gordon Lighting
Manufacturer: Modelsmith
(fabrication of custom elements).
Date Completed: May 1994
Photography: Paul Warchol

In designing offices for the rap record label Tommy Boy Music, architect Wayne Turett of the Turett Collaborative aimed to visually reconcile a sense of the company's anti-establishment, rough-edged music within the context of a corporate climate. To do so, he created a contrast between public and private spaces by using the street—the source of the music's inspiration—as a design metaphor in the corridors, while defining the offices and conference rooms as more comfortable refuges. In the corridors surrounding the warmer, more refined interior offices, the architects used raw, unrefined materials to represent an urban subtext with artful abstraction and authentic grit. Rough concrete floors like city sidewalks, concrete block dividers, and raw timber post-and-beam trellises subtly suggest the street, without making a hackneyed, commercialized imitation of it. The lighting, too, was carefully crafted to enhance the design metaphor. A series of custom-designed sconces are mounted to the rhythmic progression of trellises along one side of the corridor, creating a clever, not-too-literal impression of the dynamic quality of city lights.

Created in conjunction with lighting designer Gary Gordon, each sconce contains a triphosphor compact fluorescent lamp, covered with a custom-designed 18-inch-long sandblasted Plexiglas tube. The lamp and tube are connected to a brushed-steel ring and plate, which is bolted to a standard junction box. The box is welded to a custom-designed adjustable metal bracket, mounted to each of the many mossy green-stained raw timber trellises that punctuate one side of the corridor every six feet. To minimize the size of the sconces, remote ballasts, which service two sconces each for increased efficiency,

VENTILATION HOLE

SANDBLASTED PLEXI GLASS TUB

PL LAMP WITH UL APPROVED
PL LAMP SOCKET & HOLDER

SET SCREW
STEEL RING WELDED TO PLATE
UL LISTED ELEC. JUNCTION BOX

FLEXIBLE METAL ELECTRICAL
CONDUIT TO TRANSFORMER

CUSTOM SOLID STEEL
THUMBTURN JOINT

BENT SOLID STEEL ROD

MODIFIED STEEL ANGLES

WOOD TRELLIS

are connected to sealed tight cables extending from the sconces. Other open areas of the office echo the color and materials of these fixtures.

Collectively the sconces were designed to at once contribute to the harmony of the overall design and fulfill the lighting objectives. The mandate from the architect was to create a decorative element that would also be the sole source of illumination. The sconces provide all of the useful, diffuse, non-

directional light for the corridor, which was intended by the lighting designer to be different in quality from the more intense work lighting in the interior offices. The contrast thereby provides a visual respite.

This difference in light quality was achieved in several ways. In contrast to the uniform lighting of the interior offices, which was established with a combination of incandescent and fluorescent sources, the corridor lighting was

intentionally non-uniform, creating both dark and light areas. The level of illumination is also lower in the corridors as is the color temperature, which is about 3,000 degrees Kelvin, as opposed to 3,500 in the offices. The lamps enhance people's complexions, and also have a high color rendering index of 85. The frosted tubes have a hint of sparkle—similar to the highlights present outdoors on a sunny day—contributing to a sense of well-being. Finally, the lighting elements themselves were designed and arranged to create a sense of whimsy in the corridors, lift the spirits, and provide a sense of emotional contrast to the work spaces. By alternating the positions of the fixtures along the length of the hall, a rhythmic sense of movement visually breaks the ordered atmosphere of the offices.

The lamp life of the sconces is 20,000 hours.

SHOWROOM/EXHIBITION

CLARENCE HOUSE IMPORTS, LTD.

Location: Atlanta, Georgia

Interior Designer: Eva Maddox Associates

Lighting Designer: Patrick H. Grzybek, Eva Maddox

Manufacturers: Ceiling fixture: Norbert Belfer (low-voltage strip cove fixtures); Juno Lighting (track and PAR 30 track fixtures); Welsh Tarkington, Inc. (construction and special metal fabrications).

Date Completed: July 1993

Photography: Nick Merrick/Hedrich Blessing

Since many fabrics are intricately patterned and subtly textured, the selection and placement of fixtures and lamps are critically important. In the Clarence House Showroom in the Atlanta Decorative Arts Center, Eva Maddox Associates created a direct/indirect ceiling light system, which not only places primary emphasis on the showroom's products but visually enhances its strongly articulated coffered ceiling.

While the designers' first priority was to showcase the fabrics, they also wanted the space to be inviting and spacious for comfortable circulation and contemplation. To accomplish both objectives a synthesis of layout and lighting was key. By positioning both the direct and indirect sources along custom-designed architectural ceiling elements flanking a passage circling the space, they were able to place primary visual emphasis on the fabrics arranged on wing display assemblies against the perimeter walls, while indirectly lighting the architectural features of the ceiling above the passage itself. To avoid the common and more depressing practice of painting the ceiling a dark color, the designers raised the ceiling above the central circulation passage instead, thereby attaining the spaciousness they were after. The subtle effect produced by the indirect fixtures lighting the coffered ceiling in no way detracts from the presentation of the products.

The lighting detail consists of two primary architectural components as well as the two different light sources.

The first is an L-shaped cove and fascia extending 1 foot below the suspended sheet rock ceiling and forming the outer boundary of the passageway. The second is a free spanning stainless-steel angle, which is positioned on the interior of the passageway and set 2 inches away from the fascia so that it appears to float along the length of the passageway and punctuate its coffers. The direct lamps, 50-watt PAR 30 halogen floods, are surface mounted to the inner side of the fascia and partially concealed by the cove's lip, while the indirect lamps, low-voltage 5-watt xenon strip lights, are mounted to the upper side of the stainless-steel angle.

A track assembly was used for the PAR 30 direct sources to allow for the greatest flexibility in meeting the fixture spacing, beam spread, and aiming angle requirements for product display. The lamps were positioned 20 inches on center and their color temperature of 3,000 degrees Kelvin renders the color of the fabrics well. To accommodate energy concerns with the incandescent sources, the designers chose the more energy-efficient halogen infrared reflector lamps, which have an extended lamp-life of 3,000 to 4,000 hours. The low-voltage xenon lamps, which are connected to remote transformers and positioned 4 inches on center, appear as continuous light and were also selected to respond to energy and color temperature concerns. At 3,100 Kelvin, they are compatible with the halogen sources at reduced wattages. The average lighting load for the space is 2.5 watts/square foot.

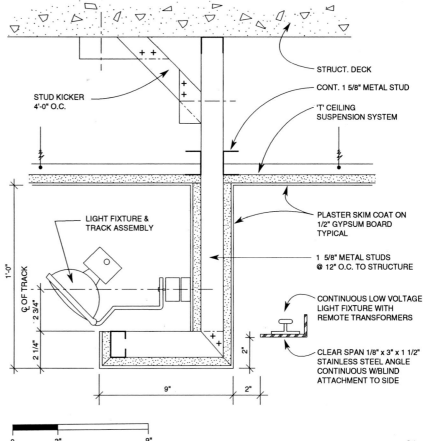

STUD KICKER 4'-0" O.C.

LIGHT FIXTURE & TRACK ASSEMBLY

℄ OF TRACK

1'-0"

2 3/4"

2 1/4"

9"

2"

2"

STRUCT. DECK

CONT. 1 5/8" METAL STUD

'T' CEILING SUSPENSION SYSTEM

PLASTER SKIM COAT ON 1/2" GYPSUM BOARD TYPICAL

1 5/8" METAL STUDS @ 12" O.C. TO STRUCTURE

CONTINUOUS LOW VOLTAGE LIGHT FIXTURE WITH REMOTE TRANSFORMERS

CLEAR SPAN 1/8" x 3" x 1 1/2" STAINLESS STEEL ANGLE CONTINUOUS W/BLIND ATTACHMENT TO SIDE

0   3"   9"

E.I. DUPONT DE NEMOURS & CO.

Location: Chicago, Illinois

Interior Designer: Eva Maddox Associates

Lighting Designer: Patrick H. Grzybek, Eva Maddox

Manufacturers: Ceiling track: Halo Lighting (track and MR-16 low-voltage halogen fixtures); Merchandise Mart Construction (custom assembly).

Date Completed: June 1991

Photography: Jon Miller/Hedrich Blessing

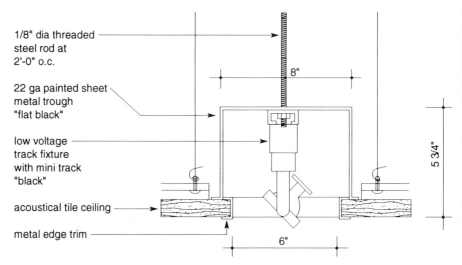

1/8" dia threaded steel rod at 2'-0" o.c.

22 ga painted sheet metal trough "flat black"

low voltage track fixture with mini track "black"

acoustical tile ceiling

metal edge trim

8"

5 3/4"

6"

It is not unusual to see standard, ceiling-mounted track fixtures used as the primary source of display illumination in showrooms. While such fixtures genuinely respond to the functional requirements of flexible and focused illumination demanded in a showroom space, frequently they are not aesthetically cohesive with the overall interior design. In the DuPont Resource Center in Chicago's Merchandise Mart, however, designers Eva Maddox Associates have taken the track fixture to a higher level by enclosing it within a minimalist recessed ceiling slot, a decision in keeping with the crisp interior architecture. As a result the space benefits from the flexibility that track fixtures provide without any visual interference in the overall design intent.

The concept is extremely simple. A prefabricated, 6-inch-wide sheet-metal trough containing a mini-track and lamp holders is recessed above and affixed to the showroom's suspended acoustical tile ceiling. The recessed track accommodates 50-watt, low-voltage MR-16s, which are fully adjustable for changing freestanding product and graphic wall displays. Used as high-level, focused accent spots on the perimeter wall (complementing an indirect fluorescent cove fixture, which provides general illumination along this wall), the MR-16s were chosen for several reasons. In addition to their adjustability, they offer added versatility because they come with a variety of reflectors, therefore providing a wide range of beam spreads to meet specific and differing

display applications. The MR-16s are also compact, which minimizes the dimensions (and visibility) of the recessed slot that contains them. At 3,100 degrees Kelvin, their whiter light offers a high color rendering capability, which is essential for product display. The MR-16s are low-voltage lamps with a lamp life of 3,000 hours, and each fixture is equipped with an individual transformer so that the track, which was wired at 120 volts, can also accommodate standard voltage lamps if desired.

While the recessed enclosure was initially developed to address aesthetic demands, it was equally considered for

functional concerns. Its dimensions, for instance, were sized to accommodate the aiming and swivel angles of the lamps. The interior of the enclosure was painted a flat black to limit the appearance of incidental light emitted from the back of the lamps, caused by their dichroic filtering. Since track fixtures are surface or pendant mounted, Chicago's building code, which requires the use of plenum-rated ceiling fixtures, does not permit their use within the ceiling. But the prefabricated sheet-metal enclosure isolates the fixtures from the plenum, thereby allowing the track fixtures to be used without violating the code.

E.I. DuPont de Nemours & Co.

Location: Chicago, Illinois

Interior Designer: Eva Maddox Associates

Lighting Designer: Patrick Grzybek, Eva Maddox Associates

Manufacturers: Auburn Plastics (sandblasted DuPont lucite cones); Dynamic Construction Co. (DuPont Corian closures); Halo Lighting (low-voltage MR-16 downlight fixtures).

Date Completed: June 1988

Photography: Jon Miller/ Hedrich Blessing

In creating a distinct visual image for the DuPont Resource Center in Chicago, architects Eva Maddox Associates used light as a primary metaphor to reinforce a message about the client's product. Located in the Merchandise Mart, DuPont's first Resource Center offers visitors the opportunity to understand the technical and aesthetic characteristics of the synthetic filaments from which its floorcoverings are made. The company is best known for a white nylon filament to which dyes are added to create a design statement. Hence, the architects translated that concept into an architectural correlative in the showroom by creating a backdrop of neutral elements to which color is added with layers of colored light rather than with paint.

While the surrounding walls of white Corian are colorfully illuminated by gelled indirect sources contained in coves, the strongest visual element underscoring the design philosophy is a series of nine translucent cones filled with colored light at the entry portal. By incorporating the option to change the color of the light permeating the cones, the design treatment also offers flexibility in its ability to complement changing displays.

The effect is achieved by projecting light from ceiling-recessed, low-voltage MR-16 halogen lamps through the translucent cones, which are made of heat-formed Lucite. The energy-efficient, whitish light from the 50-watt MR-16s is beamed through changeable colored glass lenses to alter the color of the cones, allowing them to adapt to fluctuating display requirements.

To ensure a subtle glow without excessively bright or dark spots, the inner surfaces of the cones are frosted to diffuse the colored light emanating through them. A Plexiglas mirror was located at their base to assist in obtaining uniform color and luminance throughout, returning the direct, focused beam of light from the compact fixtures back onto the diffusing inner surfaces of the cones.

The lightweight cones are seamlessly secured into the Corian-covered ceiling soffits, but are easily demounted when relamping or changing the colored lenses is necessary. A bent flange at the top of the cone is covered by a retainer disc made of Corian, which is butt-jointed against the Corian-covered surface of the soffit and secured with Allen head screws.

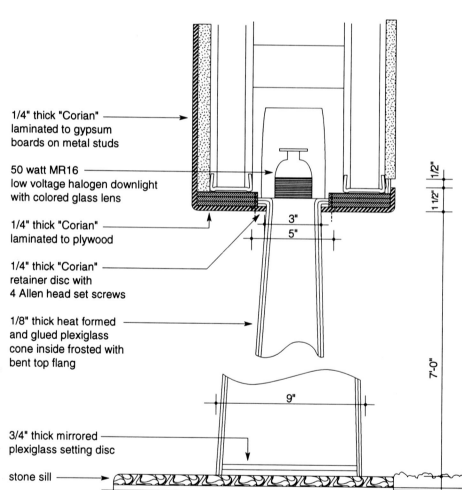

1/4" thick "Corian" laminated to gypsum boards on metal studs

50 watt MR16 low voltage halogen downlight with colored glass lens

1/4" thick "Corian" laminated to plywood

1/4" thick "Corian" retainer disc with 4 Allen head set screws

1/8" thick heat formed and glued plexiglass cone inside frosted with bent top flang

3/4" thick mirrored plexiglass setting disc

stone sill

INTERFACE SHOWROOM

Location: Chicago, Illinois

Interior Architect: The Environments Group

Lighting Designer: Joseph Connell, Environments Group

Manufacturers: 555 Manufacturing (pendant fixture); Mobile Cable Systems (aircraft cable and hardware). Wall sconce: Visa Lighting (fixture); 555 Manufacturing (fabricator).

Date Completed: May 1994

Photography: Steve Hall/Hedrich-Blessing

Detail One: Chandelier

When the contract floorcovering manufacturer Interface commissioned the Environments Group to redesign its showroom in Chicago's Merchandise Mart, its mandate to the designers was to create a space that would reflect its business philosophy. The company was essentially reinventing itself by becoming more environmentally conscious, and the designers responded by expressing the notion of editing down to basics with straightforward interior features including seating constructed of corrugated cardboard, custom fixtures made of steel with a hand-rubbed mill finish, and "crash carts" made of medium density fiberboard. Also

underscoring the "basics" theme are two minimalist lighting features which provide sophisticated illumination while aiding in the organization of the showroom's layout.

Comprising the central organizing feature in the space are a series of custom-designed pendants. Suspended from the ceiling and formally arranged over the showroom's main circulation path, the pendants suggest only the bare essence of a light fixture yet possess the sophistication of a chandelier, lending drama and sparkle to the space.

Each fixture is composed of strings of tiny incandescent lamps in porcelain sockets pooled atop a circular plate of clear tempered glass and suspended

from the ceiling by aircraft cables. To comply with a Chicago code that precludes light fixtures from being supported by a power source, the 3/8-inch-thick, 4-foot-diameter glass plate is independent of the light sources. Four strings of cable strung through the glass are anchored to the 11-foot-high concrete slab ceiling and suspend the shade 8 feet above the floor. Like Christmas tree lights, four strings containing five 15-watt A lamps each hang from a line-voltage four-plex power receptacle mounted to the ceiling and are loosely piled on top of the glass. The cords containing the lamps are UL-listed cables covered with a woven cloth insulation for decorative appeal. To keep the wires

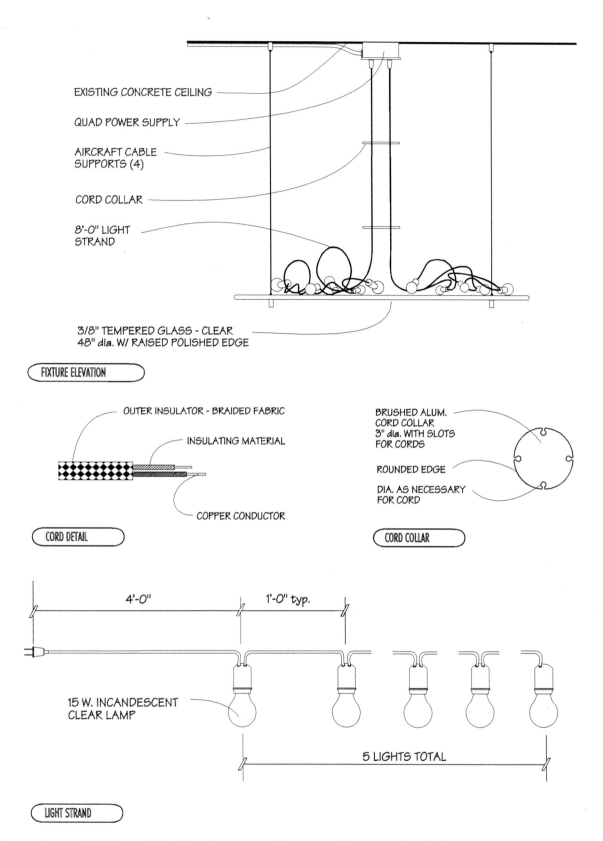

EXISTING CONCRETE CEILING

QUAD POWER SUPPLY

AIRCRAFT CABLE
SUPPORTS (4)

CORD COLLAR

8'-0" LIGHT
STRAND

3/8" TEMPERED GLASS - CLEAR
48" dia. W/ RAISED POLISHED EDGE

FIXTURE ELEVATION

OUTER INSULATOR - BRAIDED FABRIC

INSULATING MATERIAL

COPPER CONDUCTOR

CORD DETAIL

BRUSHED ALUM.
CORD COLLAR
3" dia. WITH SLOTS
FOR CORDS

ROUNDED EDGE

DIA. AS NECESSARY
FOR CORD

CORD COLLAR

4'-0"   1'-0" typ.

15 W. INCANDESCENT
CLEAR LAMP

5 LIGHTS TOTAL

LIGHT STRAND

from getting tangled before reaching the glass, they are strung through notches in two 3-inch-diameter brushed aluminum collars between the cords.

The designers chose the warmer lamps to enhance the palette of the showroom and exaggerate the texture of the floorcovering. To comply with the EPA's voluntary Green Lights guidelines to reduce energy consumption, they eventually plan to replace them with compact fluorescents once these more closely resemble the color temperature of incandescent sources. The pendants are also on dimmers and are generally dimmed by 10 percent to increase the life of the lamps.

Interface Showroom

Detail Two: Wall Sconce

Like the pendant fixtures, a series of wall sconces positioned along the two side walls of the space were custom designed with off-the-shelf components. Unlike the pendants, however, the wall sconces were developed to show the product under conditions that exist in most American corporate offices, typically a combination of direct and indirect fluorescent and ambient day light.

To create these conditions, the designers developed open areas on either side of the showroom in which to display large spans of carpet unencumbered by furniture and positioned the sconces in two locations against each wall to illuminate the floor. While the sconces were developed to simulate the effect of indirect fluorescent light, which tends to flatten texture and hide the joints between carpet tiles, tungsten halogen sources were used instead to complement the direct light of the PAR 38 lamps in the track lighting on the ceiling. The compact, high-output point sources provide ample, controlled light with a minimum of fixtures.

Each sconce consists of a wall-mounted 250-watt tungsten halogen uplight with an asymmetrical reflector positioned 30 inches below a 2-foot-wide-by-4-foot-long custom birch plywood reflector. Mounted to two brushed aluminum fins, which are bolted to a frame fastened with steel clips to the wall, the unfinished, sanded birch plywood not only complements the pared-down aesthetic of the showroom but slightly warms the cooler color temperature of the bright light source. Because the plywood is rotary cut, its natural bend allows the light reflected off it to be broadly distributed upon the expanse of carpet on the floor.

While most of the light from the sconces is thrown at a 45-degree angle away from the walls toward the reflector, it nonetheless enhances the walls' textured surface, which is coated with a hand-laid parchment technique using recycled newsprint, gesso, and tracing paper. Each row of sconces is on a separate dimmer to uniquely emphasize different products. The sconces provide approximately 50 percent of the light in the showroom.

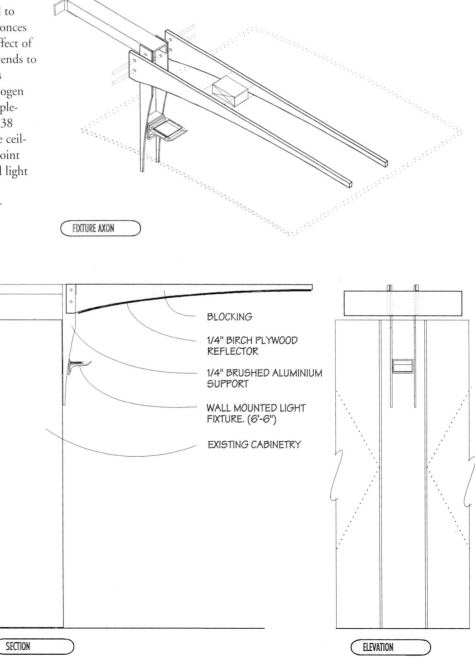

FIXTURE AXON

BLOCKING

1/4" BIRCH PLYWOOD REFLECTOR

1/4" BRUSHED ALUMINIUM SUPPORT

WALL MOUNTED LIGHT FIXTURE. (6'-6")

EXISTING CABINETRY

SECTION

ELEVATION

KENNETH COLE SHOWROOM

Location: New York, New York

Architect: Edward I. Mills & Associates

Lighting Designer: Edward I. Mills & Associates

Manufacturers: Reception ceiling slot: Newark Wire Cloth (bronze wire cloth); Legion Lighting Co. (fluorescents). Lobby light slot: Kern Rockenfield, Inc. (steel clips and angles, sandblasted glass); Legion Lighting Co. (fluorescents); Halo Lighting (quartz lamps).

Date Completed: February 1993

Photography: Chuck Choi

Detail One: Reception Ceiling Slot

The simplicity of the interior architecture by Edward I. Mills & Associates for the Kenneth Cole showroom on 57th Street in Manhattan is delicately enriched by the craftsmanship of considered yet inexpensive details. Two such details appear in the form of integrated lighting elements that accentuate the lines of the architecture with rugged sensuality.

Both of the lighting elements are recessed ceiling slots, simply and artfully shaded in two distinct manners. One of the slots appears in the reception area against the wall behind the reception desk. Remaining on 24 hours a day as part of the showroom's emergency lighting system, the light slot is 12 inches wide by 16 inches deep and runs along the length of the wall. The light potently renders the articulation of the wall, which juts out 4 inches at 18 inches below the ceiling, creating the appearance of a panel of light along the top of the wall. The fluorescent lamps are mounted to the ceiling within the slot and shaded by an undulating bronze wire cloth, diffusing and warming the cooler light.

The wire cloth shade is languidly hung on two aircraft cables strung within the slot. The cables were threaded through grommets punched through the wire cloth, connected to eyelets mounted to two steel plates on either end of the slot, and crisply buckle-tightened. The two-tube lamps were staggered to avoid socket shadows and give the effect of continuous light. The metallic shade offers an element of sparkle against the hand-plastered, ochre-colored walls, while the cooler fluorescent sources

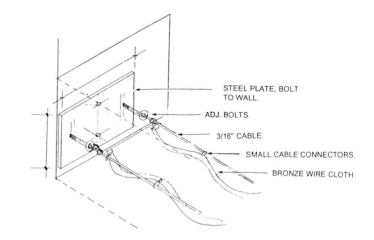

STEEL PLATE, BOLT TO WALL.

ADJ. BOLTS.

3/16" CABLE.

SMALL CABLE CONNECTORS.

BRONZE WIRE CLOTH.

DETAIL: END CONNECTION
11/2"= 1'-0"

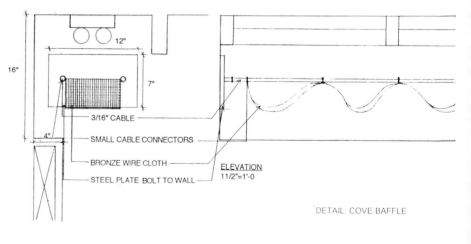

12"

16"

7"

3/16" CABLE

SMALL CABLE CONNECTORS

4"

BRONZE WIRE CLOTH

STEEL PLATE BOLT TO WALL

ELEVATION
11/2"=1'-0

DETAIL: COVE BAFFLE

SECTION : END CONNECTION.
11/2"=1'-0"

Kenneth Cole Showroom

behind the shade accentuate the hints of bluish pigment in the plaster and contrast with the warmer surfaces of the sandblasted maple desk and its burnished hot-rolled steel desk top.

Detail Two: Lobby Ceiling Slot

The light slot designed by architect Edward I. Mills in the entrance lobby of the New York Kenneth Cole showroom integrally ties the lobby to the showroom on the other side of a pivoting glass door. Referred to by the architect as a linear chandelier, the light slot runs along the entire length of the lobby ceiling and visibly extends through two vertical clear glass panels in the lobby walls to the areas on either side of the lobby.

In contrast to the undulating bronze wire cloth shade over the light slot in the showroom's reception area, the lobby light slot is covered by randomly layered 1-foot-wide panes of sand-blasted glass, which vary in length from 3 to 7 feet. By varying the number of overlapping layers of glass along the slot, the light emanating from the ceiling-mounted fluorescent lamps above penetrates the glass at differing levels of intensity and creates an interaction of shadows with diffuse light, evoking the qualities of a chandelier. The glass is sandblasted on one side and placed face down for ease of maintenance.

The panes of overlapping glass are supported within the 18-inch-wide-by-2-foot-deep ceiling slot by angled clips of hot-rolled steel rods welded to steel angles bolted to the interior fascia of the slot. The angles and rods punctuate the slot with dashes of darkness against the long band of light. Two bands of sandblasted glass cap the panes of glass at either end of the slot as end plates.

In addition to functioning as a source of illumination, the light slot plays an important role in an interplay of linear architectural elements at the juncture between the lobby and the showroom. The dividing line between these two areas is defined by four floor-to-ceiling features: a 4-inch-wide slot against the perimeter wall, a 1-foot-wide fin wall, an 18-inch-wide clear glass panel, and a 9-foot-wide, etched-glass pivoting door. The light slot completes this medley of linear forms as the horizontal transverse extension of the vertical clear glass panel sandwiched between the fin wall and pivoting door.

The 4-, 6-, and 8-foot-long, 10-watt/foot fluorescents were staggered to offer the appearance of continuous light. The average light load for the project is about 2 watts/foot.

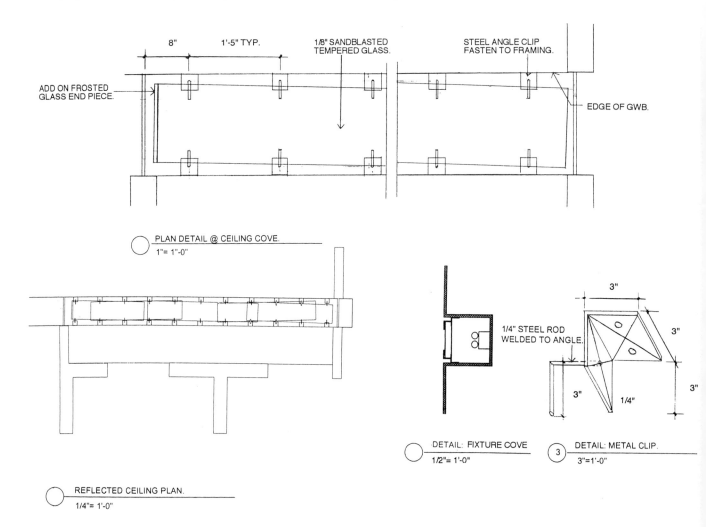

ADD ON FROSTED GLASS END PIECE.

8"   1'-5" TYP.   1/8" SANDBLASTED TEMPERED GLASS.   STEEL ANGLE CLIP FASTEN TO FRAMING.

EDGE OF GWB.

PLAN DETAIL @ CEILING COVE.
1"= 1'-0"

1/4" STEEL ROD WELDED TO ANGLE.

3"

3"

3"

3"

3"   1/4"

DETAIL: FIXTURE COVE
1/2"= 1'-0"

DETAIL: METAL CLIP.
3   3"=1'-0"

REFLECTED CEILING PLAN.
1/4"= 1'-0"

THE KNOLLGROUP SHOWROOM

Location: New York, New York

Interior Designer: Haigh Architects, Paul Haigh and Barbara H. Haigh

Lighting Designer: Paul Haigh

Manufacturers: National Lighting (fluorescent lamp); Kern/Rockenfield (metal work); GE Plastics (extruded Lexan Thermoclear diffuser).

Date Completed: October 1992

Photography: Elliott Kaufman

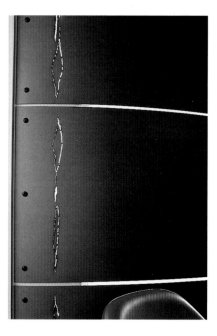

In his second interior renovation and expansion of the KnollGroup's furniture showroom in New York, architect Paul Haigh addressed architectural problems he hadn't solved 10 years earlier. His primary concern was concealing a stairwell which extends from the ground floor of the open loft space to the office areas above. To negate the volumetric intrusion of the stairwell into the space, the architect concealed it with a curved wall—echoing the boat-shaped form of the classic conference table designed by Florence Knoll and defining part of a new conference area on the other side. A lighted sculptural steel extension connected to the curved wall accentuates its graceful line and complements the showroom's industrial material aesthetic and detailing, which is expressed most boldly in product backdrop panels of steel plate and rolled aluminum plate window displays.

The sculptural extension is actually composed of five 5½-foot-long-by-2-foot-7-inch-wide curved panels of oxidized steel mounted to the wall at one end and connected to a floor-to-ceiling pole at the other. The panels are separated by 1/4-inch-wide slits and articulated by a vertical irregular pattern burnt through the steel. A shaft of vertical light integrated within a cove at the edge of the wall illuminates the panels on one side and bleeds through the slits and patterned articulation on the other.

The 14½-foot-high-by-6¼-inch-wide vertical cove is fitted with two 6-foot-long, 60-watt warm-white fluorescent lamps, and covered by a panel of ribbed extruded Lexan Thermoclear to diffuse the light and produce a slightly striated effect on the surface of the steel panels. Painted white, the interior surface of the cove reflects the light. The ribbed diffuser covering the lamps is mounted to a piano hinge on one side, pulling open for easy access to the lamps. A magnetic catch secures the diffuser into place when closed. The warm-white fluorescents were selected to enhance the oxidized quality of the steel and complement the warmth of the PAR 56 tungsten lamps suspended from the ceiling throughout the space.

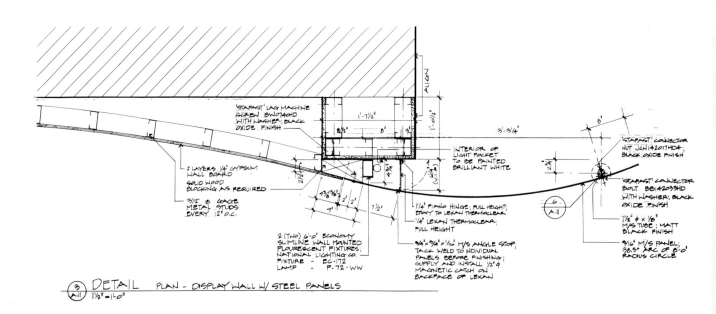

UNITED CHAIR SHOWROOM

Location: Chicago, Illinois

Interior Designer: Tom Gass

Lighting Designer: Theo Kondos Associates

Manufacturers: Pendant luminaires: Kramer Lighting (pendant luminaire); Lightolier (lampholders); GE (PAR 38 spots). Conference room wall lights: Sylvania (PAR 30 spots).

Date Completed: June 1991

Photography: Jon Miller/Hedrich-Blessing

Detail One: Pendants

In his design for the showroom of furniture manufacturer United Chair at the Merchandise Mart in Chicago, interior designer Tom Gass cast a theatrical tone, envisioning the space as dark with the product showcased in light. Though the showroom's ceilings are relatively high, the emphasis is on the floor where four groupings of chairs are spotlighted from custom-designed pendant luminaires whose flexible structure and high-tech form add to the stage-set atmosphere. Another light source, punctuating the base of a curved interior conference room wall in the showroom, keeps the eye oriented toward the floor and accentuates the wall's sweeping form. Aside from their role as sources of illumination, both fixtures serve as sculptural elements that reinforce the overall design.

The overscaled pendants, created in conjunction with lighting designers

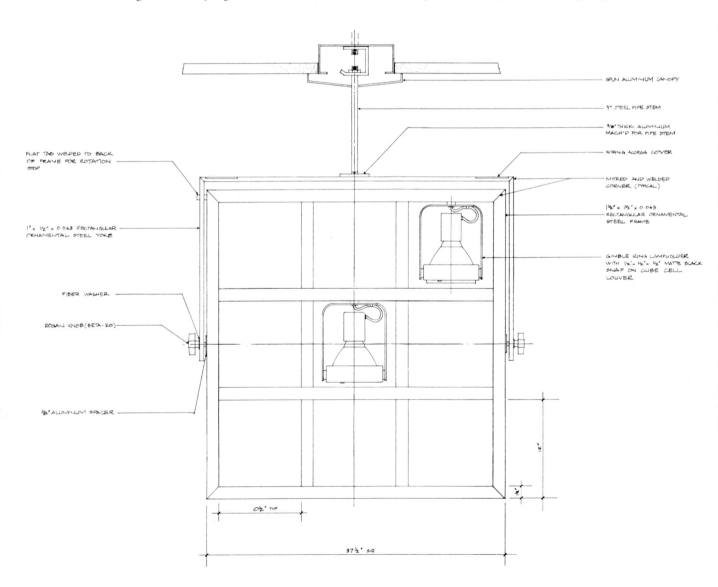

SPUN ALUMINUM CANOPY

9" STEEL PIPE STEM

3/8" THICK ALUMINUM MACH'D FOR PIPE STEM

WIRING ACCESS COVER

MITRED AND WELDED CORNER (TYPICAL)

1½" x 1½" x 0.063 RECTANGULAR ORNAMENTAL STEEL FRAME

GIMBLE RING LAMPHOLDER WITH ½"x ½"x ½" MATTE BLACK SNAP ON CUBE CELL LOUVER.

FLAT TAB WELDED TO BACK OF FRAME FOR ROTATION STOP

1"x ½" x 0.063 RECTANGULAR ORNAMENTAL STEEL YOKE

FIBER WASHER

ROGAN KNOB (BETA-20)

⅛" ALUMINUM SPACER

12"

10½" TYP

37½" SQ

United Chair Showroom

Theo Kondos Associates, were designed not only to light the product but also to visually tie together the groupings of chairs. Their industrial quality is coupled with a dynamic construction, allowing their multiple light sources to be precisely focused on the merchandise. Though dominant in scale, the black pendants recede into the raw concrete slab ceiling, which is also painted black, again to reinforce the emphasis on the floor. The pendants are gridded steel frames containing nine 90-watt PAR 38 quartz spotlights in gimble ring lampholders that allow them to be adjusted to a variety of angles. The designers created the bold yet humble frame not only to complement the standard light fixtures it holds, but to reflect the solid, robust nature of the region in which the showroom is located.

Like the fixtures, the frame itself is adjustable. It is attached to a steel yoke via Rogan knobs, which allow it to be rotated and positioned to the angle most appropriate for lighting the furniture. The yoke is suspended from the ceiling by a 9-inch-long steel stem, whose connection at the ceiling is concealed by a spun aluminum canopy. The pendants are wired from the ceiling through the steel stem, into the yoke, and threaded through the gridded steel frame to the individual fixtures. The yoke contains two wiring access covers in the event repairs are necessary.

The chiaroscuro design concept is heightened by a series of deliberate graphic elements, including inset carpet patterns of stripes and circles in tuxedo-like black and white. The theatrical spotlight effect of the ceiling fixtures is enhanced by the large white circular patterns located beneath each chair in the groupings of furniture.

Detail Two: Apertures
Unlike the ceiling fixtures, which accentuate the furniture and graphic components of the design, the lighted

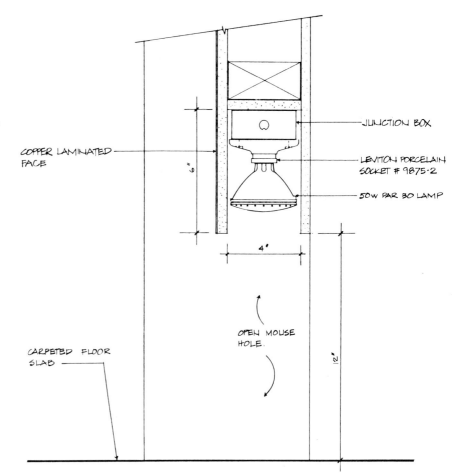

rectangular apertures at the base of the curving conference room wall are detached from the graphic system so as not to compete with the furnishings, yet they offer relief to the wall. Instead of functioning as dominant design elements as the pendants do, the "mouse holes" are subtler design intonations with their lighting components hidden from view.

Each of the five 1-foot-high-by-9-inch-wide openings at the base of the wall is highlighted from above by a 50-watt PAR 30 flood lamp contained within a pocket inside the wall. The lamps are mounted in the 6-inch-deep recess to a porcelain socket attached to a junction box wired through the wall.

While these light features do not compete visually with the graphic components of the design, they do reinforce the designer's intention of anchoring the focus on the floor. The apertures' 1-foot height appropriately calls just enough attention to the base of the wall by keeping the level of illumination emanating from the sources above them low, while meeting the code requirement for access allowance. Both the "mouse holes" and the pendants emphasize Gass's talent for celebrating details as well as his knack for imaginative design when the budget is limited and his design objectives are high. His innovative use of the most basic of standard fixtures has brought deepened dimension to the showroom design.

UNITED CHAIR SHOWROOM

Location: Los Angeles, California

Interior Designer: Tom Gass

Lighting Designer: Theo Kondos Associates

Manufacturers: Ceiling fixture: Universal Manufacturing Corp. (steel truss); Stonco (lampholders); Lighting Services Incorporated (sparkle hoods, 290 Series fixtures); GE (PAR 38 spots); String fixtures: Sirrah (Garbo string fabric); GE (PAR 30 lamps).

Date Completed: February 1990

Photography: Toshi Yoshimi

Detail One: Ceiling Fixture

One of the essential strategies interior designer Tom Gass uses in creating showrooms is to devise design elements that draw visitors into the space. In his design for the United Chair showroom at the Pacific Design Center in Los Angeles, two such elements are lighting treatments, both of which pull the eye through the long expanse of the rectangular space and serve to link the display environment to the product.

The first element, designed in conjunction with lighting designers Theo Kondos Associates, reinforces Gass's inclination to tie his designs to their location, in this case both the building and Los Angeles. Supporting a mild aquatic theme, the fixture is actually a skeletal ceiling structure, which, accord-

ing to the designer, elicits the effect of the "belly of a whale" and plays on the Pacific Design Center's nickname, "Blue Whale." The structure consists of a 40-foot-long spinelike metal truss that supports a series of riblike bent metal conduits with spot lights attached to their ends. The industrial quality of the fixture contrasts with the romantic quality of the showroom's architectural elements and finishes, particularly the gentle wave pattern in the carpeting. Yet the curving lines of the fixture's metal conduits soften the contrast and complement the rolling sense of movement created by the carpet patterns in tandem with a series of cul-de-sacs on either side of the showroom in which the products are located.

The individual strips of standard industrial conduit were bent off site and

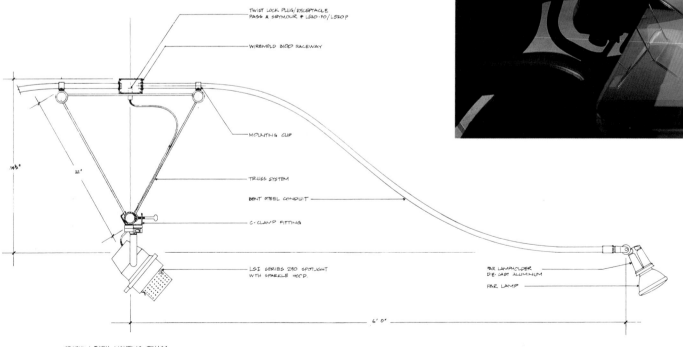

TWIST LOCK PLUG/RECEPTACLE
PASS & SEYMOUR # L520-FO/L520P

WIREMOLD 3100 RACEWAY

MOUNTING CLIP

TRUSS SYSTEM

BENT STEEL CONDUIT

C-CLAMP FITTING

LSI SERIES 290 SPOTLIGHT
WITH SPARKLE HOOD.

PAR LAMPHOLDER
DIE-CAST ALUMINUM

PAR LAMP

6'0"

SECTION THRU LIGHTING TRUSS

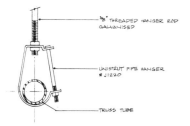

assembled on site so that the lamps could accurately accent the products inside the eight cul-de-sacs on either side of the room. Clamped to the metal truss, which is suspended from the ceiling by steel cables attached to custom hangers, the conduits are connected to a wiremold raceway running along the top of the spine. Both the 150-watt PAR 38 quartz spots connected to die-cast aluminum lamp holders at the end of the conduits and those in the adjustable 290 Series fixtures fitted with sparkle hoods and suspended from the base of the triangular truss by standard C-clamp fittings were selected for their color rendering qualities. At 3,050 degrees Kelvin, the quartz lamps, accenting the products and offering ambient light, have the highest color rendering index of any incandescent source.

Detail Two: Lighted Dividers

The other notable lighting treatment, a series of wedge-shaped, light-filled translucent "screens" dividing the cul-de-sacs in which the products are displayed, also supports the aquatic atmosphere of United Chair's L.A. showroom. These multi-purpose forms emphasize the product with additional light and serve as quasi-architectural elements that separate one product from another while their translucency allows a misty view through the space.

The light-filled forms are simply floor-length string curtains made of parachute cords, attached to fabric strips and hung with Velcro from the triangular recesses in a soffit surrounding the perimeter of the showroom. They are lighted from above by a row of three 75-watt PAR 30 quartz flood lamps mounted to a wire raceway within the recess. Tiny holes drilled into the recess allow heat to escape, but are so small that light is kept from illuminating the ceiling. The reflective sheen of the wall-covering on the soffit creates a halo of light around each form, and the overall effect is doubled by walls of mirrors on either side, which turn the wedge-shaped light forms into diamonds when viewed head on.

The lamps are connected to a dimming system that allows the forms to be further manipulated. When the lights are dimmed the curtains become more translucent; when the lights are bright they become more opaque. By changing the color of the lamps the "screens" can be adjusted to coordinate with changing displays and enhance different colors of upholstered chairs.

All of the lighting in the space is compliant with California's Title 24 code for energy efficiency, illustrating the designer's budget-conscious knack for making something out of nothing with theatrical imagination.

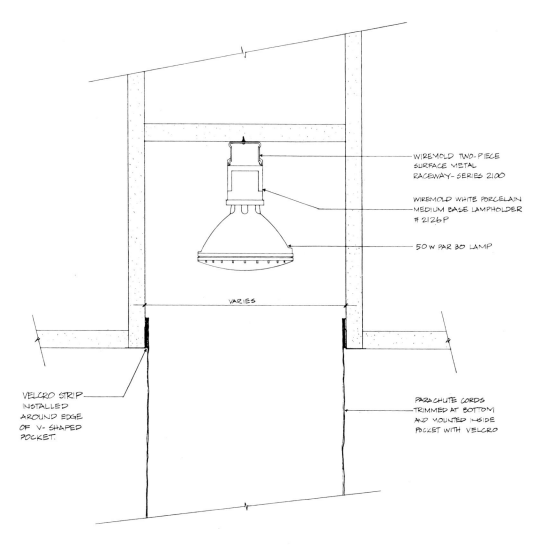

WIREMOLD TWO-PIECE SURFACE METAL RACEWAY- SERIES 2100

WIREMOLD WHITE PORCELAIN MEDIUM BASE LAMPHOLDER #2126P

50 W PAR 30 LAMP

VARIES

VELCRO STRIP INSTALLED AROUND EDGE OF V-SHAPED POCKET.

PARACHUTE CORDS TRIMMED AT BOTTOM AND MOUNTED INSIDE POCKET WITH VELCRO

VECTA

Location: New York, New York

Interior Designer: Lee Stout, Inc.

Lighting Designer: Lee Stout

Manufacturers: Legion Lighting (fluorescents); Lightolier (AR-70 track fixtures); Rosco (gels); American Louver (ceiling egg crate); Osram (lamps).

Date Completed: October 1991

Photography: Elliott Kaufman

While displays may change, most everything else in showrooms stays the same. In the Vecta furniture showroom in New York, however, interior designer Lee Stout used a very simple lighting technique to create colorful shifts in atmosphere for seasonal variety or special parties.

Integrated within raised display platforms throughout the space, colored light emanating from coves beneath the platforms' surfaces is reflected on vertical backdrops behind the furniture. Several staggered 4-foot-long standard fluorescents, surface-mounted to a stringer within the troth below the platform and concealed by an extended lip of the platform floor, are covered with gels of various colors and project diffuse light toward the wall. A polished 1/16-inch-thick aluminum reflector, friction-fitted between the fluorescent fixture and a J channel at the back of the cove, reflects the colored light up along the wall, creating an ombrÈ effect as it fades near the top.

The interior elements in the space are either black or white to adapt to any color gel used on the lamps. The gels are selected to complement the furniture on display, which is illuminated from the front by 50-watt AR-70 adjustable quartz lamps suspended from a long-stemmed track along the ceiling. The tracks, along with the air-conditioning duct, sprinklers, and emergency lighting are all concealed by an egg-crate ceiling grid. Only the lamp heads protrude through the grid and are aimed at the furniture.

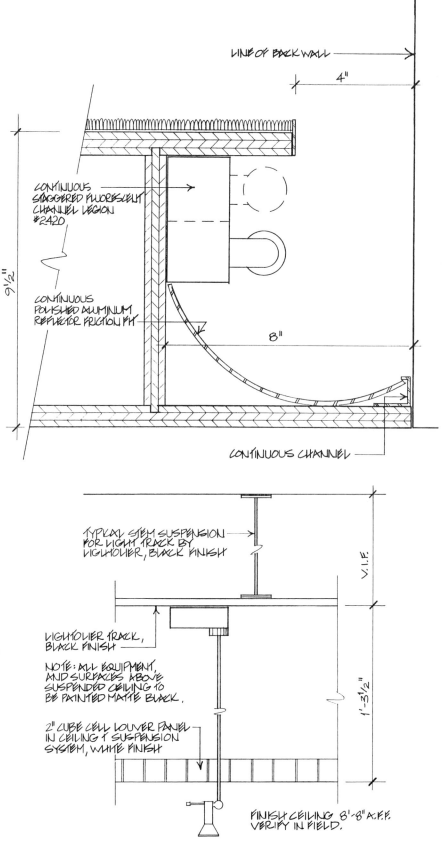

HOSPITALITY

BAANG

Location: Greenwich, Connecticut

Interior Architect: Rockwell Architecture, Planning, and Design P.C. (Rockwell Group)

Lighting Designer: Rockwell Group

Lighting Consultant: Focus Lighting

Manufacturers: Sylvania (PAR-20 lamps); Modeworks (copper screen); Rick Lee of Kamikaze (copper-clad columns and yoke mountings).

Date Completed: February 1995

Photography: Paul Warchol

In his design for a French-Chinese restaurant called Baang in Greenwich, Connecticut, architect David Rockwell emphasized the cultural collision of the restaurant's cuisine with a vibrant composition of color, material, and form. While the two cultures are suggested through the vivid palette of ginger root yellows and chili pepper reds, the energy that comes from the fusion of these cultures is expressed in a collection of explosive columns of light randomly punctuating the space.

Composed of plywood enclosures clad with a patchwork of oxidized copper plates, the angular columns start narrow at their bases, flare outward at the tops, and are capped by huge floating sail-like scrims, creating pockets of vertical energy throughout the open, loftlike space. Wrapped around existing steel columns, each copper-clad enclosure appears as an irregular cone within a cone. In recesses at the top of the lower cone four 50-watt PAR-20 flood lamps accentuate the upward thrust of the column with soft, diffuse light,

while yoke-mounted adjustable MR-16s in the upper cone punch out focused light across the 8-foot-wide-by-12-foot-long sail-like copper screen, grazing it with shimmering light. The MR-16s are fitted with two types of lenses: a linear spread lens, which sharpens the beam and directs the light vertically or horizontally, and a diffusion lens, which powders the light and makes it soft and fuzzy. The copper-brown ceiling recedes from view, allowing the shimmery screen to stand out in contrast.

Though essentially decorative, the light columns nonetheless provide substantial illumination, supplemented by additional MR-16 downlights focused on each table. The PAR-20 flood sources were chosen for their even intensity, white light, and clarity. They were also chosen for their good color rendering capability and chromaticity, which is similar to that of the MR-16s. Transformers for the MR-16s are located at the base of the columns and all of the lamps are on dimmers.

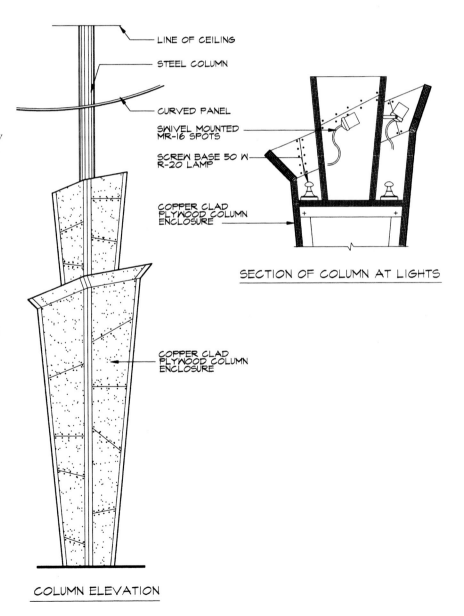

LINE OF CEILING

STEEL COLUMN

CURVED PANEL

SWIVEL MOUNTED MR-16 SPOTS

SCREW BASE 50 W R-20 LAMP

COPPER CLAD PLYWOOD COLUMN ENCLOSURE

COPPER CLAD PLYWOOD COLUMN ENCLOSURE

SECTION OF COLUMN AT LIGHTS

COLUMN ELEVATION

CAROLINE'S COMEDY CLUB

Location: New York, New York

Interior Designer: Haigh Architects with Paul Haigh and Barbara H. Haigh

Lighting Designer: Paul Haigh

Manufacturers: Fiber optics: Fiberstars (MR-16 lamp, color wheel, and fiber optic tube). Ceiling fixture: Halo Lighting (fixtures); Sylvania (MR-16s); Glass & Mirror Craft (tempered glass panels); Kern Rockenfield (metal work); Lutron Electronics (Versaplex dimming system).

Date Completed: May 1992

Photography: Elliott Kaufman

Detail One: Fiber Optics

When Caroline's Comedy Club moved from its South Street Seaport location to midtown Manhattan on Broadway, its owner wanted the new venue to provide more than laughs. A dining room and cozy lounge area for intimate drinks were included in the program, and Haigh Architects were enlisted to design the cavernous basement space with its 18-foot-high ceilings and concrete walls. They created a rich neo-Medieval atmosphere with velvet, tapestry, and harlequin motifs that not only establish an inviting air of comfort in the heart of Times Square, but recall the street theater and performances of the Renaissance. Lighting plays a key role in enhancing and articulating the architects' design objectives.

Among the many lighting elements employed, fiber optics are one of the most significant. Added to outline architectural features and define circulation paths, fiber optics also complement the space's colorful palette. In a passageway to the rest rooms, for instance, two narrow bands of fiber optic light enhance a forced perspective the architects created by tapering the ceiling height from 10 feet at the start of the passage to 8 feet in front of the rest room doors.

At the junction between the wall and the ceiling, the 1/2-inch-diameter fiber optic tubes are set into 3/4-inch-high reveals on both sides of the passageway. Fastened into extruded plastic clips, they are illuminated by a single 250-watt

MR-16 illuminator focused with a special lens and adapter and concealed above the ceiling. The lamp is also screened with a color wheel, which gradually cycles the light through magenta, green, aqua, and white filters and subtly echoes the vibrant colors of the rich

upholstery and harlequin-patterned, aniline-dyed Finnish birch plywood paneling. Ribbons of fiber-optic light integrated into the banquettes in the theater accentuate their curved lines, as well as highlight the curved fascia soffit defining the bar and bar area in the lounge.

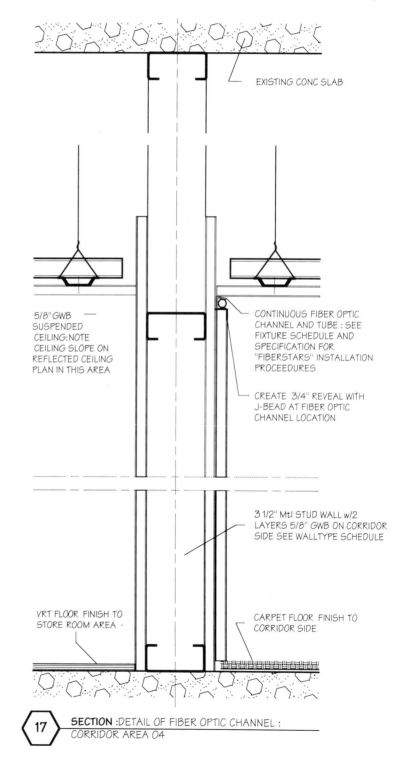

EXISTING CONC SLAB

5/8" GWB SUSPENDED CEILING: NOTE CEILING SLOPE ON REFLECTED CEILING PLAN IN THIS AREA

CONTINUOUS FIBER OPTIC CHANNEL AND TUBE : SEE FIXTURE SCHEDULE AND SPECIFICATION FOR "FIBERSTARS" INSTALLATION PROCEEDURES

CREATE 3/4" REVEAL WITH J-BEAD AT FIBER OPTIC CHANNEL LOCATION

3 1/2" Mtl STUD WALL w/2 LAYERS 5/8" GWB ON CORRIDOR SIDE SEE WALLTYPE SCHEDULE

VRT FLOOR FINISH TO STORE ROOM AREA ·

CARPET FLOOR FINISH TO CORRIDOR SIDE

17 **SECTION** :DETAIL OF FIBER OPTIC CHANNEL : CORRIDOR AREA 04

Disney Contemporary Resort Hotel and Convention Facility

Detail Two: Decorative Grid Light

In contrast to the millwork fixture in the prefunction corridor, the lighting located in the translucent windows of the rotunda is strictly decorative. During the day, general illumination is provided by a large overhead skylight. At night, an uplight cove around the skylight's interior vertical surface, incandescent wall washers on the surfaces without window grids, and ceiling-mounted downlights light the area. The decorative light in the gridded wall not only sparkles and glows, but also serves as an interesting motif when viewed from the exterior of the atrium building complex.

The rotunda's geometry—established by a cylindrical volume of space and a checkerboard floor pattern—is reinforced by the pattern created on its lighted interior grid wall. The wall was built to contain a series of 51 2-foot-square windowed cubes, within each of which is placed a single 40-watt incandescent candelabra lamp. The lamps are mounted in a custom-designed, white-painted aluminum tube, which rises from the base of the hollow metal window frame surrounding the cube. A circular aluminum plate extending from the tube and concealing the light source from direct view creates the impression of a circle floating within the glowing cube of light. Four tiny squares punched into the face of the plate allow the brighter light near the diffuse source to emanate through, creating a series of sparkles in the center of the glowing box.

Each of the cubes is glazed with a plane of 1/4-inch-thick, translucent laminated glass, which is secured by flush removable stops. All exposed surfaces are painted white to match the windows in the rest of the project. Painted drywall and acoustical panels are positioned between the cubes for a gridded effect. The lamps, which are connected to a junction box in the base of the window box and to a timer so that they are illuminated only at night, are dimmed by 40 percent for warmer color and increase their lamp life to about 8,000 hours.

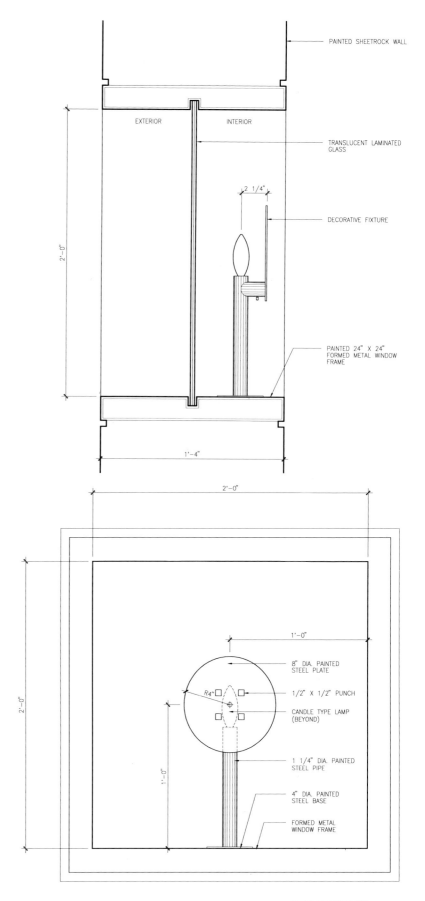

THE FOUR SEASONS HOTEL

Location: New York, New York

Architect: Pei Cobb Freed & Partners Architects

Associate Architect: Frank Williams & Associates

Interior Architect: Chhada, Siembieda & Partners

Lighting Designer: Fisher Marantz Renfro Stone

Manufacturers: Wall sconce: CSL Lighting (fabricators); Philips (A-19 lamps); Lightolier (fixture in lower arm); Philips (PAR 20 lamps); CSL Lighting (extruded aluminum channel); Sayegh International Co. (Pakistan white onyx). Ceiling lights, lobby lounge: GE (MR-16 NSP lamps, downlights); Osram (AR-111 PAR 36 lamps); GE (MR-16 adjustable floods). Wainscoting uplight, lobby lounge: CSL Lighting (fabricators); Philips (reflector lamps); CSL (metal housing, wireway). Uplight, piano bar: CSL Lighting (fabricators); Philips (R20 reflector lamps); CSL (wireway). Exterior lanterns: CSL (fabricator); Philips (compact fluorescents); GE (PAR 56 VNSP downlights); Jerome Extrusion (aluminum housing and structure).

Date Completed: October, 1993

Photography: Peter Paige and Peter Vitale

Detail One: Entrance Foyer

Conceived in the spirit of such New York landmarks as the Chrysler Building and the Waldorf Astoria, the Four Seasons Hotel on 57th Street in Manhattan promises to join in their ranks as a modern classic. Designed by architect I.M. Pei of Pei Cobb Freed & Partners, with interiors by Chhada, Siembieda & Partners, the hotel blends contemporary luxury with Art Deco style, embodied in pared-down elements and gracious detailing. Among the design features are numerous lighting details which enhance the elegant ambiance and serve as potent extensions of the architecture.

Completed just before the April 1994 Federal Energy legislation was passed, the Four Seasons is probably one of the last big buildings to be illuminated primarily with incandescent light. While the warmth of these more expensive sources complements the hotel's interior palette of bronze, cognac, and champagne tones and enhances the air of luxury established by the materials—limestone, marble, Danish beechwood, and onyx—the overall lighting scheme, created in collaboration with lighting designers Fisher Marantz Renfro Stone, was driven by long-term operational costs and maintenance concerns. Hence, the increased up-front costs of these fix-

tures is offset by their low-wattage and extended lamp-life via connection to a pre-timed dimming system.

The integration of lighting and architecture is immediately apparent in Pei's soaring grand entrance foyer, where the eye is drawn toward two enormous, custom-designed, 6½-foot-tall wall sconces flanking the central staircase and a ceiling laylight above. Both the wall sconces and ceiling are shaded with 3/8-inch-thick panes of onyx. Aside from their decorative function, the sconces serve two purposes: they provide general ambient illumination and offer focused accent light on potted plants placed below them.

Given the owners' operational and maintenance requirements and the architects' material mandate, the lighting designers developed an electrical lamp component that responded to all of the functional and aesthetic demands. In order to provide light that would be compatible with the colors, materials, and atmosphere of the project, the lighting designers chose 25-watt A19 incandescent lamps for their soft, white, diffuse qualities, which minimize reflection in the specular surface of the onyx ceiling laylight above. Concerned with the opacity of the onyx, they determined that the stone had to be at least 25 percent transmissive in order to permit enough light to pass through it to be

LEGEND:

1. Extruded aluminum mounting plate
2. Extruded aluminum incandescent socket strip
3. Lamp: 25W A-19/W
4. 120 V receptacle
5. Removable power cord for relamping
6. Release latch for relamping
7. Extruded cover plate
8. Extruded aluminum channel with integral guide for installation and alignment
9. Architectural lantern reference
10. 2-Lamp "Y" socket
11. Extruded aluminum wireway
12. J-box
13. Adjustable PAR 20 accent light (in architectural bracket arm)
14. Junction box/grounded outlet (for light strip)
15. Die cast aluminum housing
16. Lamp: G.E. 50W PAR 20
17. Yoke lock
18. Adjustable yoke
19. Junction box

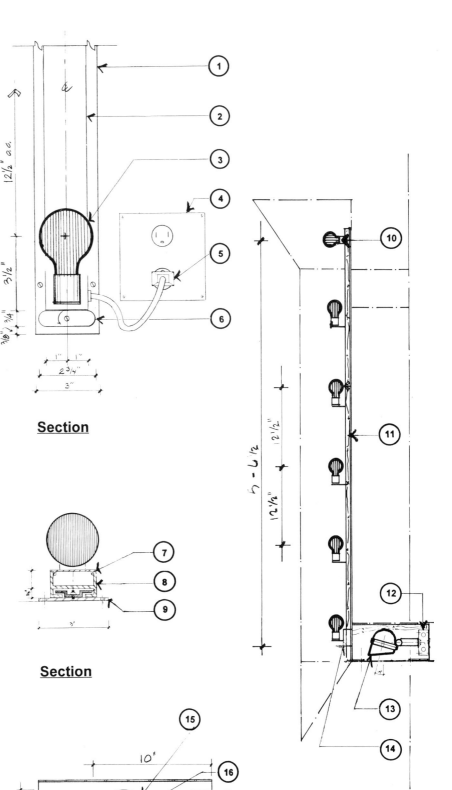

Section

Section

Section

Section

effective. After testing several samples they recommended the white Afyon onyx from Pakistan. In order to evenly illuminate the tall sconce and respond to the maintenance concerns, the lighting designers side-mounted six A19 lamps to a 5½-foot-long, custom-designed extruded aluminum channel, which, with a turn of a release latch, simply slides out when relamping is necessary.

To provide accent light for the potted plants below the sconce, the lighting designers mounted an adjustable 50-watt PAR 20 lamp to the junction box at the base of the channel beneath the bracket arm. The PAR 20 offers a focused beam of light, creating shadow play and highlights in the plant's foliage. The adjustable lamp is locked into place so that the lamp may be changed without altering the focus.

Detail Two: Recessed Ceiling Light

In the elevated lobby lounges flanking the grand foyer, two lighting treatments discretely blend with the interior architecture and subtly establish a more intimate atmosphere. Here, again, aesthetic effects were tantamount to maintenance concerns. In illuminating the inverted coffered ceiling, for instance, two primary objectives guided the lighting treatment. The first was the architects' desire to have as narrow an interstitial grid between the ceiling panels as possible without interruption by large downlight fixtures. The second was to avoid the necessity of relamping from below since the lounge areas were to be operational 24 hours a day.

The lighting designers created a 3-part ceiling light strategy using minimal apertures in the grid and a catwalk system above the ceiling to allow for relamping. While the code in such an area typically demands a 4-inch aperture for standard downlights, the top lamping strategy allowed for a 3-inch aperture. A family of three different lamp types in the ceiling fulfills the different illumination requirements of the space. Most of the apertures are fitted with 75-watt narrow spot MR-16 direct downlights for general illumination. Over the floral displays, 100-watt AR-111 PAR 36 lamps provide accent light, and 75-watt MR-16 adjustable floods fitted with spread lenses illuminate the walls.

Since the MR-16 floods do not light the wall all the way up to the ceiling they are not true wall washers. To fine tune the beam, they are fitted with an adjustable yoke and a black-finished anodized-aluminum reflector cone that

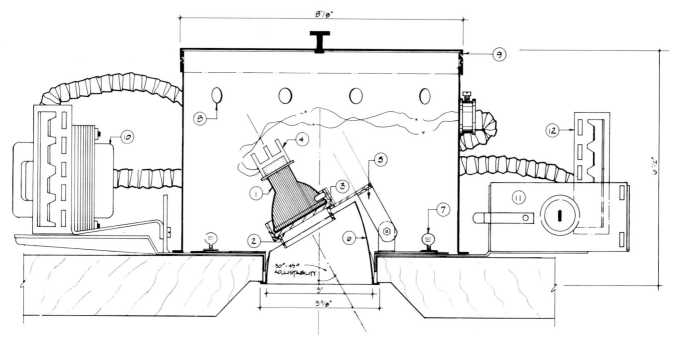

Section

LEGEND:
1. Lamp: 75W MR-16 FL
2. Spread lens
3. Lamp holder
4. Miniature Bi-pin socket
5. Adjustable yoke
6. Cone: Specular anodized aluminum black finish
7. 360∞ rotation lock
8. Ventilation hole
9. Housing cover (removable for relamping)
10. Transformer: 120V-12V magnetic step down type
11. Junction box
12. Ceiling mounting hardware

TEMPEST

Location: Houston, Texas

Interior Designer: Jordan Mozer & Associates

Lighting Designer: Jordan Mozer & Associates

Manufacturers: Jordan Mozer & Associates (general contractor); Craft Metal Spinnings (bowl spinnings); Toolco Inc. (machining of spinnings); Platers Polishers (polishing); Janeen Art Studio (degreasing and finishing); Olma Glass (glass blowing); Around the Stained Glass (acid-etching); Ace Rubber Hose Co. (neoprene grommets); Wagner Bronze Foundry (bronze brackets casting); Toolco Inc. (machining); Griffin Co. (polishing); Barclay Marine (hardware); Annexter Wiring Cable (cable); McMaster-Carr (ceiling hardware); Tech Lighting Inc. (electrical components).

Date Completed: October 1992

Photography: Chas McGrath

In a Houston restaurant/nightclub called Tempest, Chicago designer Jordan Mozer draws on the parallels between what happens in a nightclub and the turn of events in Shakespeare's great play by the same name. According to the designer, the metaphor aptly describes the goings on in a club, where the musical, magical mysteries of the night transform the tedium of the work day into a promise of liveliness or a chance for love. Mozer's visual realization of these ideas is expressed in lush, ripe forms, and his idiosyncratic take on Shakespeare's magic has just the right mix of theatrical drama and all-American frontier imagination to make both a literary genius and Lone Star urban cowboy feel at home.

All of the custom-designed elements in this space illustrate the lengths to which the designer goes to produce his unique ideas. After envisioning a series of ceiling light fixtures, which look like spiky tumbleweeds or wind-whipped lonesome stars, for instance, Mozer personally took on the role of contractor in manufacturing special lamp shades to create the right effect at the right price. By keeping the custom-fabricated pieces separate from the electrical elements he was also able to produce them to meet commercial codes without requiring UL approval.

Organized around a radial plan—central to the recurring theme of "restaurant as theater" in Mozer's designs, and which, in this case, symbol-

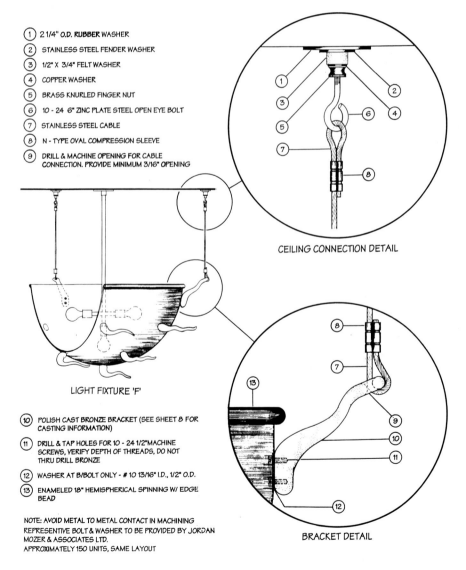

1. 2 1/4" O.D. RUBBER WASHER
2. STAINLESS STEEL FENDER WASHER
3. 1/2" X 3/4" FELT WASHER
4. COPPER WASHER
5. BRASS KNURLED FINGER NUT
6. 10 - 24 6" ZINC PLATE STEEL OPEN EYE BOLT
7. STAINLESS STEEL CABLE
8. N - TYPE OVAL COMPRESSION SLEEVE
9. DRILL & MACHINE OPENING FOR CABLE CONNECTION. PROVIDE MINIMUM 3/16" OPENING

CEILING CONNECTION DETAIL

LIGHT FIXTURE 'F'

10. POLISH CAST BRONZE BRACKET (SEE SHEET 8 FOR CASTING INFORMATION)
11. DRILL & TAP HOLES FOR 10 - 24 1/2"MACHINE SCREWS, VERIFY DEPTH OF THREADS, DO NOT THRU DRILL BRONZE
12. WASHER AT B/BOLT ONLY - # 10 13/16" I.D., 1/2" O.D.
13. ENAMELED 18" HEMISPHERICAL SPINNING W/ EDGE BEAD

NOTE: AVOID METAL TO METAL CONTACT IN MACHINING
REPRESENTATIVE BOLT & WASHER TO BE PROVIDED BY JORDAN MOZER & ASSOCIATES LTD.
APPROXIMATELY 150 UNITS, SAME LAYOUT

BRACKET DETAIL

izes both the eye of the storm and the enchanted island where the action of the play is carried out—the custom light fixtures bring the doughnut-shaped room to life. His typically dense detail is only part of what makes his forms come alive, however. The effect of motion is usually built into his designs so that the architecture appears to dance, accelerate, or, in this setting, blow around in the buffeting wind. The columns bend and curve as though pushed by a gusty gale, while other ceiling lights, shaped like long-forgotten boot boxes, look as if they just drifted in after blowing around for miles.

The tumbleweed fixtures, 20 in all, are actually a series of cauldron-shaped, spun-copper "canopies," ranging in diameter from 9 to 60 inches and perforated with holes through which tentacle-like spikes of blown glass protrude, as if twisting and turning in blustering winds. The spun-copper cauldrons mask commercially rated, inexpensive, ceiling-mounted conduit stems to which 60-, 75-, or 100-watt incandescent bulbs are attached, depending on the size of the canopy. Light eerily emanates through the glass spikes, which were acid-etched to soften the glow. In order to suspend the fixtures from the ceiling, each is

equipped with three or four sand-cast bronze brackets, which are attached by hidden bolts to the canopy shell. One-foot-long strips of phosphor bronze cable (standard sailing hardware) were looped at both ends, connected to the bronze brackets, and suspended from open-eye bolts in the ceiling. To support the weight of the canopies, which weigh up to 100 lbs., the hardware of the ceiling connections is attached to fire-treated plywood planks. The planks were placed in the roof cavity above the ceiling's two layers of drywall to reinforce the ceiling and distribute the load.

Barneys New York

2-foot-long T-8 fluorescent lamps are mounted on either side of the negative space behind each box and emit light toward the niches where the perfume is displayed, while heat is distributed through the back of the case. The lamps, which emit light at 3,000 degrees Kelvin, were chosen for their high color rendering capability, their ability to provide even illumination, and their energy efficiency. Also, the lamps offer ample illumination without a lot of wattage or heat, which is important since perfume is sensitive to light and temperature.

Additional uplight illumination is provided by 10-inch-long, 18-watt biaxial, high-output compact fluorescent lamps. These are mounted in the center of a glass-covered hardwood enclosure recessed in the counter beneath each niche along the bottom row of boxes. The 1/4-inch-thick glass is frosted to create a soft smooth glow of light. The lighting designers also recommended that the bottoms of smaller display cubes, often placed within the niches, be left open and their tops covered with the 1/4-inch-thick frosted glass to allow the light to channel through. Small holes were drilled through the base of the enclosure to allow for heat ventilation.

Special attention was given to controlling the light in a number of ways. For instance, because the lamps provide more illumination than is actually necessary, the recessed pockets were designed to be 9 inches deep to keep the fixtures hidden, blocking a fair amount of the light. Additionally, while the light heightens the glamour of the platinum-leaf finish on the back wall, the specularity of this surface demanded that it be coated with a matte lacquer to limit excessive reflection. Steel light shields were bolted to the tops and bottoms of each recess to keep light from seeping through the cracks. The inner walls of the cavity below the display cubes were painted matte white to diffuse the light and avoid the spotty effect produced by light reflected off natural wood.

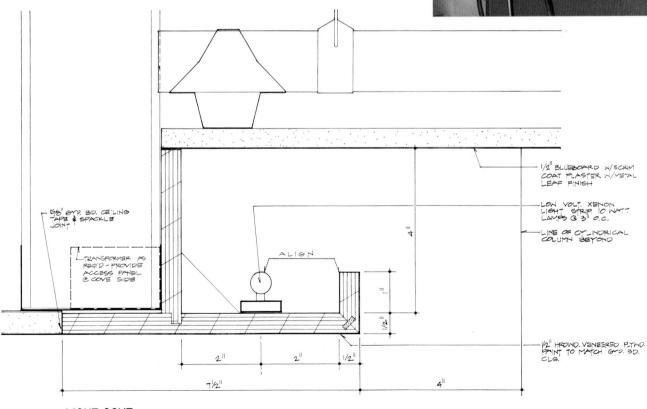

LIGHT COVE

Detail Two: Ceiling Cove

A ceiling cove created by Johnson Schwinghammer in Barneys' women's shoe department also enhances the glamour of another metallic finish—in this case, gold leaf on the ceiling. The architect wanted to create the uplit ceiling cove to define the shoe department with an architectural form that would distinguish its identity from the other selling areas on the fourth floor. Doing so was difficult, however, because of a low ceiling height of only 8 feet. The area also called for particular attention to illumination since it was the only part of the floor that wasn't adjacent to the windows.

Typically, a ceiling cove can range between 10 to 20 inches deep, but here the lighting designers had to create the shallowest cove possible—only 4½ inches deep. As a result, only the use of low-voltage fixtures was possible since the lip to hide the fixtures could only rise to 1½ inches in height and still allow enough room for relamping. To complement the gold tones of the ceiling as well as the warm, creamy palette of the furnishings, the lighting designers chose to use 10-watt xenon lamps, which, at 2,800 degrees Kelvin, emit a yellow light that would enhance the ceiling and surroundings.

In order to respect the clean lines of the interior architecture, the cove seamlessly melds with the suspended ceiling. This was achieved by perfectly aligning the 1/2-inch-thick plywood base of the cove with the 1/2-inch-thick blueboard ceiling (used because it would readily accept the scrim coat plaster and gold-leaf finish). On the side of the ceiling that is seen, the point at which the plywood meets the blueboard was taped and spackled and the base of the plywood cove was painted to match the ceiling finish. On the hidden side of the ceiling, the two surfaces are joined by a metal U angle that is bolted to aluminum studs rising behind the cove.

Because the fixtures are low-voltage, enough room had to be built in behind the cove to accommodate a transformer, which rests in the cavity above the metal angle behind the cove. The strip fixtures are centrally placed on the base of the cove and spaced 3 inches on center, creating the illusion of a band of candlelight. Though at 40 watts/linear foot, the energy efficiency of this strategy is not at a maximum, its effect evokes the glimmering golden age of the 1930s, as the architect intended, with ingenuity and economy of material in a most limited space.

Barneys New York

Detail Three: Ceiling Cove

A third lighting detail created by Johnson Schwinghammer in the women's section softly illuminates the products and interior surfaces of the apothecary department on the main floor. As in the women's shoe department a ceiling cove was used, and like the merchandise in the perfume department, the products here are extremely sensitive to light and heat. But the execution of the lighting detail is unique to the conditions of this setting.

The apothecary area is filled with temperamental products, many of which are packaged in materials made with natural vegetable dyes that easily fade under harsh light. The area is also defined by a mosaic frieze with imagery adapted from the Roman/Byzantine designs of those at Ravenna. Low-heat, low-watt fluorescents were chosen for the ceiling cove to prevent damage to the light- and heat-sensitive products. To establish a fresh, clean, antiseptic quality of light appropriate to such an atmosphere the lighting designers covered the cove light with thick white case glass to whiten the cool, 3,500-degree Kelvin light of the fluorescents, while diffusing it to keep it from becoming harsh and sterile. The horizontal lines of the ceiling cove also

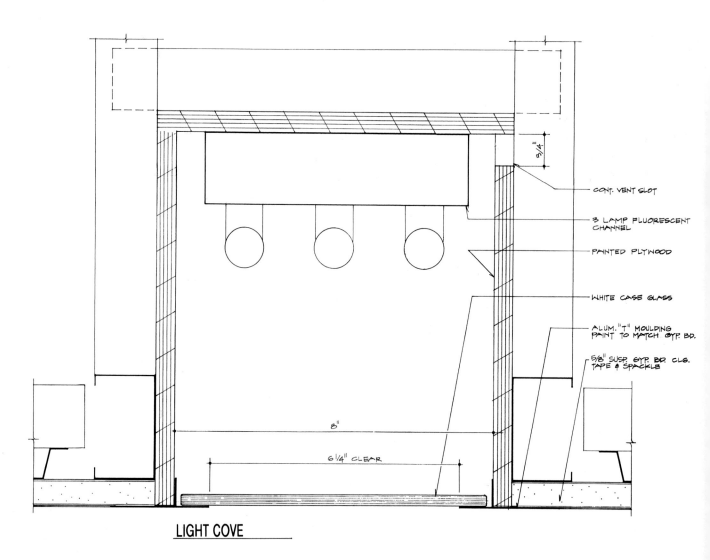

3/4"

CONT. VENT SLOT

3 LAMP FLUORESCENT CHANNEL

PAINTED PLYWOOD

WHITE CASE GLASS

ALUM. "T" MOULDING PAINT TO MATCH GYP. BD.

5/8" SUSP. GYP. BD. CLG. TAPE & SPACKLE

8"

6 1/4" CLEAR

LIGHT COVE

accentuate the length of the frieze. The cove light is also supported in illuminating this architectural detail by a series of tiny, shielded wall washers fitted with 50-watt, low-voltage bi-pin halogen lamps.

In order to simplify and minimize the presence of the cove in deference to the intricate mosaic, the lighting designers opted to keep the ceiling plane as pure as possible by creating a cove that is virtually flush with it. A series of 2-, 3-, and 4-foot-long, 3-lamp fluorescent channels are mounted in the 8-inch-wide-by-10-inch-deep cove set into the ceiling 2 feet away from the frieze. Aluminum T-moldings extend from the sheet rock ceiling and form the lip upon which the white case glass rests. The T-molding is taped to blend imperceptibly with the ceiling.

The careful treatment of the glass was most critical in creating the pure effect of this cove. In order to keep the socket shadows of the fixtures (which are mounted end to end) from being visible, 1/4-inch-thick, water-white, white cased glass covers the cove and diffuses the light, allowing it to appear as a soft, clean, continuous band. The 20-foot-long cove was covered with several 8-foot-long plates of glass, which meant that the points at which the separate plates of glass meet also posed the risk of interrupting the purity of its continuous band of light. In order to keep these points invisible, the lighting designers requested that the glass be cut to fit on site and butt-jointed into place. Access to the lamps is made possible by tip-tilting the glass and lifting it out.

BULGARI

Location: New York, New York

Architect: Piero Sartogo, Architetti Associati

Lighting Designer: H.M. Brandston and Partners

Manufacturers: Recessed soffit lights: Leviton (A lamps). Ceiling beam uplight fixtures: Lucifer lighting (halogen strip fixtures). Jewelry vitrines: Lightolier (MR-16 track and track fixtures); Lightolier (spread lenses).

Date Completed: October 1991

Photography: Norman McGrath

Detail One: Recessed Light Features

Seemingly carving recesses in the ceiling and walls of the Bulgari jewelry store in New York, broad bands of light articulate the serene space with glowing warmth, while a ribbon of highlighted jewelry vitrines wraps around the store like a sparkling bracelet. Though the combined effect complements the store's luxury, the real beauty of this lighting is its utter simplicity. Designed by architect Piero Sartogo, the Bulgari store is a labyrinth of sumptuous materials and finishes, and the lighting of these elements by H.M. Brandston and Partners

enhances their inherent qualities and classical execution. The 3-inch-thick, hand-rubbed plaster ceiling, for instance, is accentuated by two different lighting techniques that not only bring out its texture but call attention to its vaulting form.

In the soffits facing the carved ceiling recesses, rows of square open cavities—plastered inside with the same European technique used on the ceiling—are simply fitted with single, 100-watt, frosted A lamps emitting soft, warm light in all directions. The depth of the cavities was determined by sightlines so the lamps would remain unseen from the floor,

while their square forms echo the rectilinear shapes of the vitrines below.

In contrast, recessed within narrow slots in the ceiling beams over the portals leading to other areas in the store, are two low-voltage strips of 10-watt, frosted bi-pin halogen uplights with reflectors, spaced 2⅛ inches on center. These fixtures accentuate the ceiling with a whiter light than that of the standard A lamps in the soffit cavities. To allow the vitrines to be the real focus of attention, however, the uplights were slightly dimmed.

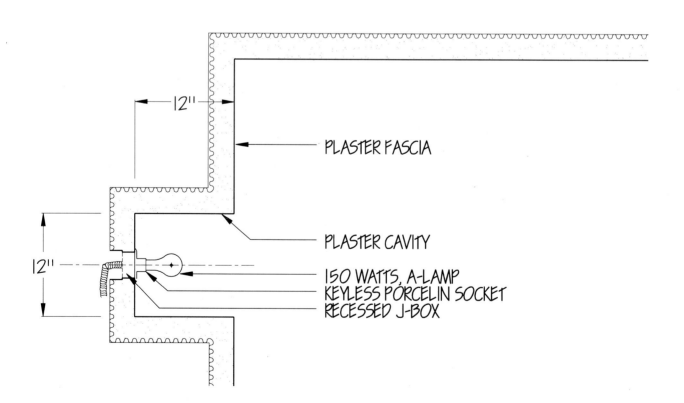

FELISSIMO

Location: New York, New York

Interior Architect: Clodagh Design International

Lighting Designer: Johnson Schwinghammer Lighting Consultants

Manufacturers: Torcheres: Fiberstars (fiber-optic cables); Philips (HID luminaire); FiberStar (luminaire box). Minstrel's gallery bridge: Osram (AR-70 spot); Norbert Belfer (fixture).

Date Completed: October 1992

Photography: Daniel Aubry

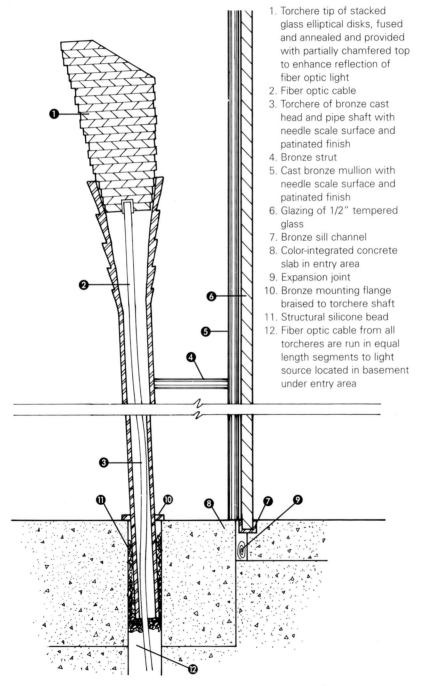

1. Torchere tip of stacked glass elliptical disks, fused and annealed and provided with partially chamfered top to enhance reflection of fiber optic light
2. Fiber optic cable
3. Torchere of bronze cast head and pipe shaft with needle scale surface and patinated finish
4. Bronze strut
5. Cast bronze mullion with needle scale surface and patinated finish
6. Glazing of 1/2″ tempered glass
7. Bronze sill channel
8. Color-integrated concrete slab in entry area
9. Expansion joint
10. Bronze mounting flange braised to torchere shaft
11. Structural silicone bead
12. Fiber optic cable from all torcheres are run in equal length segments to light source located in basement under entry area

Detail One: Torcheres

Felissimo, an upscale eco-emporium designed by Clodagh with architect Robert Pierpont, is a quirky mix of environmentally conscious hand-wrought elements, both old and new. Located in a midtown-Manhattan, six-story Neo-Classical townhouse designed by Grand Central Terminal architects Warren & Wetmore in 1901, it is richly detailed with the work of more than 50 artists, designers, and craftspeople, including 85 custom-made fixtures and furnishings, which together meld into a stylistic amalgam of Mediterranean, Japanese, and industrial intonations. Among the many details that inspire the senses in this shop are several custom-designed lighting elements—some of them artisan-crafted fixtures, others standard fixtures integrated into the architecture or furniture. Two of the most notable examples are a series of torcheres flanking the shop's entrance and a haunting lighted glass bridge in the minstrel's gallery on the mezzanine.

Standing sentinel on either side of the store's entrance, three pairs of "reeded flower fixtures" invitingly call attention to the store's frosted glass doors, etched with windblown fossil-like fronds. Hand-crafted by artist Jay Gibson, each torchere is composed of a slender, reed-like cast-bronze base topped by a knob of fused stacked glass. The bronze and

glass echo the bronze-mullioned windows on either side of the entrance, as well as the hand-cast bronze door pulls on the etched-glass entrance doors. The materials and motif of these fixtures are also repeated inside in the form of a fiber-optic newel post at the base of a bronze-coated Rococo stair rail.

Working with lighting designers Johnson Schwinghammer, Clodagh opted to use fiber-optic lighting in the torcheres for a number of reasons: It has a brilliance that stands up to daylight and provides a glow on a gray day; it is cool to the touch; and is as free of van-dalism as possible. The lighting designers selected a 150-watt HID lamp as a point source for each of the two illuminator boxes, which are remotely located in the basement, and connected three 1/2-inch-diameter fiber-optic cables at each of their ports. To protect the cables threaded through the bronze bases, the lighting designers specified that they be wrapped in a black PVC sleeve, which is coated white on the inside. The white coating redirects the light traveling through the cable back onto itself so that it is as bright as possible when it reaches its destination. After mocking up the torcheres with the artist, the lighting designers also suggested that the perimeters of the glass cones be sawed at jagged angles to create a faceted sparkle. Through the glass, the light projected along the fiber-optic cables creates a cool shimmering aqua glow, in sharp contrast to the warm bronze bases and ochre-stained limestone facade.

Though more expensive to install, the fiber optics are cheaper to operate. The lamp life of the sources illuminating these fixtures is approximately 6,000 hours.

Felissimo

Detail Two: Minstrel's Bridge

Echoing the etched-glass doors at Felissimo's entrance is the glass floor of the minstrel's gallery on the store's mezzanine. In designing Felissimo, Clodagh chose to preserve as much of the original structure as possible on the two lower floors, while making a more modern statement on the upper floors. Located between the second floor and the third, the minstrel's gallery is a transition area that presages the unique spaces on the floors above. According to Clodagh, the mezzanine presented the opportunity for a "moment to go wild," and the frosted-glass floor, which comes alive with light shining through it, creates a mysterious mood of enchantment.

The mezzanine's lighted floor is a metaphor for the light one finds in nature. Like dappled sunlight through a leafy tree, the light projected through the glass floor was consciously designed to be uneven. To create the effect, lighting designers Johnson Schwinghammer

positioned several 50-watt halogen AR-70 spot lamps along one side of the glass floor, creating a strong burst of light that gradually bleeds off as it reaches the middle. The shadowed quality desired by the designer is enhanced by the nature of the floor itself. Its 1-inch-thick panes of glass are frosted and etched on the underside with little icons by artist David Johnson, and divided by bands of stainless steel and concrete.

The placement and inherent qualities of the lamps were also key in producing the effect. Hidden behind copper-coated metal panels which conceal the HVAC system, the lamps are mounted to an extruded aluminum raceway and positioned 5 inches on center. According to the lighting designers, the halogen sources were used for several reasons. Their precise 10-degree beam spread allowed the light to be focused directly through the glass, and their light output level of 19,000 lumens/watt was sufficiently high to drive the light through

the density of the glass. Additionally, at 3,200 degrees Kelvin, their whitish color complemented the clear etched glass. And because they are filament lamps, the light they produce creates a sparkling clarity, which enhances the qualities of the glass rather than diminish them as a linear fluorescent would. Connected to a remote transformer, their lamp-life is 2,000 hours, and they are accessed through a removable face plate from below.

Designed to be energy sensitive, all of the lighting at Felissimo was considered for its cumulative wattage. It was also designed to be flexible and easy to maintain. While the details presented here are fixed, other lighting elements, such as the custom-designed ceiling pod system, were developed to be easily moved and redirected toward the ever-changing displays. The total lighting load is 2.3 watts/square foot, below the state energy code of 2.4 watts/square foot.

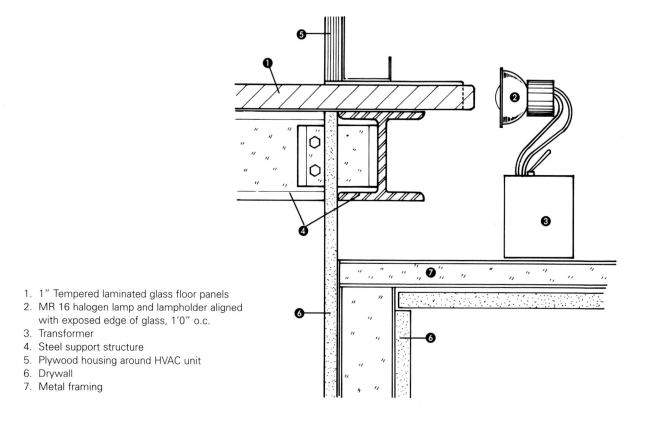

1. 1″ Tempered laminated glass floor panels
2. MR 16 halogen lamp and lampholder aligned with exposed edge of glass, 1'0″ o.c.
3. Transformer
4. Steel support structure
5. Plywood housing around HVAC unit
6. Drywall
7. Metal framing

JIL SANDER BOUTIQUE

Location: Paris, France

Interior Architect: Gabellini Associates

Lighting Designer: Johnson Schwinghammer Lighting Consultants

Manufacturers: Vitrines: Philips (fluorescents); Modular International (halogens); Modular International (recessed ceiling fixtures); Modular International (dichroic filters). Dressing room uplight: Philips (350-watt halogen); Johnson Gabellini (custom fixture). Stair slot: Philips (fluorescents); Elliptipar (reflector and bracket).

Date Completed: March 1993

Photography: Paul Warchol

Detail One: Display Vitrines

Designed by Gabellini Associates, the Jil Sander clothing boutique, housed in a landmarked 19th-century building in Paris, was conceived of as a virtual stage set. Given his background in theatrical design, architect Michael Gabellini focused on light as a central consideration in his overall concept for the space. In fact, contrary to the way in which

space is usually conceived, the boutique was essentially organized around how it would be lighted. After stripping away the interior's extraneous layers and surface decoration, a more monolithic sense of space and proportion was revealed, influencing the architect's spatial configuration of the of the space. Ultimately, the entire space was defined as a neutral background, a series of

frames within a frame. Each of these frames contains the clothing and accessories, which are emphasized as the central "characters" of this particular drama. Their lead role is accentuated and intensified through the conscious manipulation of light within the individual frames, distinguishing them with color or brightness and allowing the monolithic architectural elements around them to recede as background features.

Created in conjunction with lighting designers Johnson Schwinghammer, the lighting concept encompasses three areas: the series of vitrines in which the clothing is displayed; a series of more intimately scaled dressing rooms; and the sculptural stairwell. The light visually defines all of these areas as the primary points of activity. Against the mostly horizontal, monolithic planes of architecture, these spaces read similarly as vertical slots of light. Though each is lighted differently, mostly indirect lighting techniques were used to sculpt and mold these individual areas.

The negative volumes within the display vitrines are washed in a "veiled haze" of light. Three separate sources were used to define the volume and accentuate the clothing in the vitrine. A concealed 8-watt/linear foot, high-color-rendering fluorescent reflects off the vitrine's interior surfaces, filling it with a diffuse, veiled haze of light. Next to the fluorescent is an adjustable 75-watt halogen flood lamp, whose 10-degree beam spread is completely contained within the vitrine and is focused downward on the merchandise. At 3,000 and 3,200 degrees Kelvin respectively, the

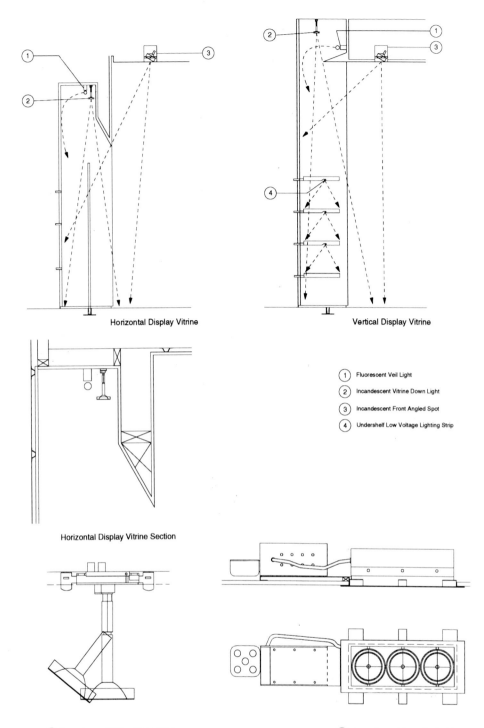

Horizontal Display Vitrine

Vertical Display Vitrine

1. Fluorescent Veil Light
2. Incandescent Vitrine Down Light
3. Incandescent Front Angled Spot
4. Undershelf Low Voltage Lighting Strip

Horizontal Display Vitrine Section

2. Incandescent Vitrine Down Light

3. Incandescent Front Angled Spot

two lamps were chosen for both their high color-rendering capability and for their virtually imperceptible difference in color. Finally, a series of adjustable, ceiling-recessed halogen fixtures are positioned in front of the vitrine, casting direct light on the front of the merchandise. All of these fixtures (except the fluorescents) are dimmed at various levels to balance with the incoming light from morning to night. They are also colored with various dichroic filters—depending on the merchandise—to em-

phasize the character and mood of a particular collection.

The light level in the vitrines—much brighter than the ambient light level in the remainder of the space—strongly distinguishes them as display spaces. Illuminated with 100 footcandles of light, the volume within each vitrine is decidedly higher than the 25 footcandles of reflected light on the surrounding surfaces. Enhancing this effect are the vitrines' blemish-free plaster surfaces finished with a satin titanium white

paint, which is the most reflective paint available. The direct light hitting the surfaces inside the vitrine is amplified and evenly distributed, while the walls framing the vitrine go flat under the indirect ambient light. The fixtures inside the vitrine are mounted as close to the inner vertical surface as possible, to avoid producing a hot spot on the back wall and to hide the lamps from direct view. A customized cross-hair baffle on the interior halogen fixture also diminishes glare.

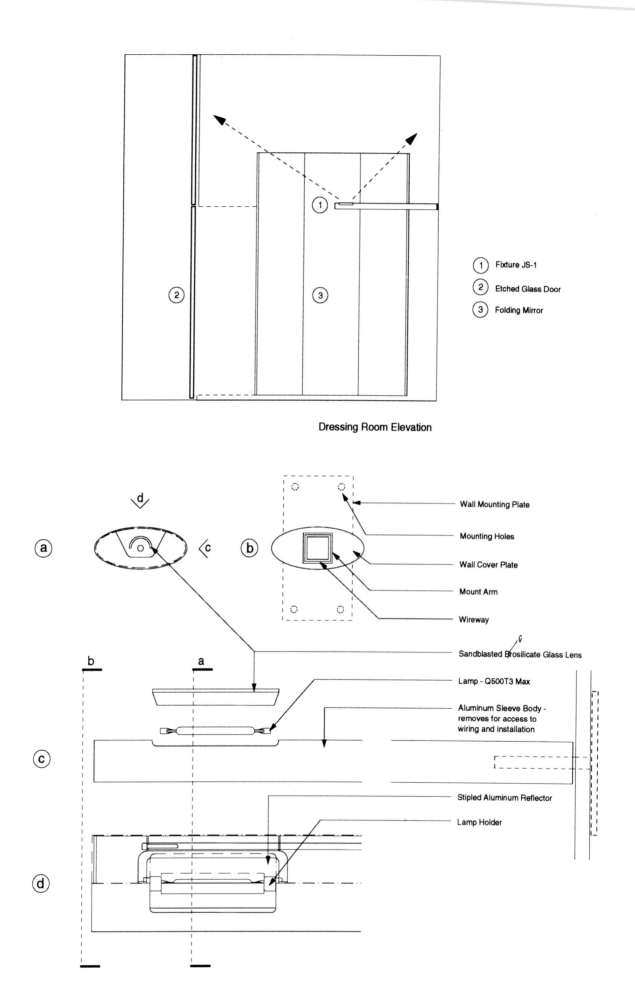

Dressing Room Elevation

1. Fixture JS-1
2. Etched Glass Door
3. Folding Mirror

Wall Mounting Plate

Mounting Holes

Wall Cover Plate

Mount Arm

Wireway

Sandblasted Brosilicate Glass Lens

Lamp - Q500T3 Max

Aluminum Sleeve Body - removes for access to wiring and installation

Stipled Aluminum Reflector

Lamp Holder

Detail Two:
Dressing Room Uplight

Like the display vitrines, the reflected light emanating through the etched glass doors of the dressing rooms appears misty and in shafts. However, the effect is achieved here by filling the rooms with indirect light from a powerful uplight source, contained within an elegant custom fixture. Gabellini opted to use an uplight fixture not only to fulfill his spatial objective of creating a shaft of reflected light, but to avoid the unflattering shadows that are cast by direct light. To fill the 8-by-10-foot space with light, an energy-saving 350-watt halogen lamp with a lumen output level equivalent to a 500-watt source was used. Dimmed to only 2/3 of its full wattage for the proper effect, the 3,200-degree-Kelvin lamp was chosen for color consistency with other lamps and for its high color-rendering capability. The fixture containing the single lamp is positioned next to a mirror at a point halfway between the floor and the 15-foot-high ceiling. Like the vitrines, the interior surfaces are finished with a blemish-free plaster painted satin titanium white, to evenly reflect and distribute the light.

The fixture itself is a 3-foot-long, oval-shaped shaft of painted aluminum. Designed with a female connection at one end, it is mounted on a solid-metal post male connection, attached to a steel plate behind the wall. The lamp is positioned in a removable lamp holder, containing a stippled aluminum reflector at the other end of the aluminum sleeve. The reflector was designed for wide light distribution away from the wall to avoid shadows and hot spots and to throw off heat so that the sleek skin of the fixture would not have to be perforated for ventilation. Atop this assembly is a sandblasted borosilicate glass lens, which diffuses and evenly distributes the light. The architect chose the oval shape for the fixture both for its geometric beauty and because the reflected light

rolls off its surface, in effect dematerializing the form.

Within the dressing room the volume is filled with reflected light above the fixture, creating a diffuse, soft white light; below the fixture, the light is refracted. From outside the dressing room, through the etched glass door, an even shaft of light appears to pulsate into the public space beyond. The door is an etched optical water-white glass, which in effect reacts to the light like a large refracting lens. Unlike the cold light that penetrates through ordinary glass, the diffused light coming through

the lead-free water-white glass is warm, intimate, and soft. The architect's intention was to create the feeling of being in a courtyard, echoing the classic 19th-century tradition of the French courtyard expressed in neighboring buildings.

Outside the dressing room, an identical fixture is also positioned next to a floor-to-ceiling monolithic mirror—a literal metaphor that extends the idea of reflection. A series of these fixtures are staggered in other parts of the public space as well, to break up the coolness of the architectural planes that are in the shade.

Jil Sander Boutique

Detail Three: Stair Slot

Complementing the smaller vertical shafts of light in the Jil Sander boutique and further articulating its spare volume are three monolithic vertical architectural elements. The most significant of these is the marble-clad rectilinear enclosure surrounding the grand winding staircase. The staircase, itself a dynamic structural tour de force partially revealed from the entrance through a slot in the enclosure, cascades through the space like a fanned deck of cards. Adjacent to this slot, another slender slot of light, recessed in a corner of the enclosure, enhances the sense of dynamic energy and movement created by the staircase in the pure, serene space, and rises through all four stories of the store.

The purpose of the light is twofold. When viewed from the outside, it highlights the separation between the plaster and marble masses on either side of the slot that reveals a hint of the staircase. From the inside, it illuminates the interior volume of the staircase chamber with indirect light, and accentuates the staircase's architectural detailing. Conceptually, the effect is created in a manner similar to that of the vitrines, but a different source of light is used. Surface-mounted end to end within the carefully designed recess are eight 5-foot-long fluorescent fixtures equipped with arced reflectors, which scoop the light out of the slot and direct it toward the stairwell. Remote ballasts preclude the need to stagger the lamps, which produce the effect of a continuous 40-foot-high band of reflected light. Though mounted on swivel brackets, once the precise placement of the lamps was determined in order to achieve the desired effect, they were permanently locked into place.

The lamps are shielded from view by a plaster fin projecting from the outer edge of the recess. After several mock ups, the architect and lighting designers determined that the fin should be set at a 45-degree angle to partially illuminate the stairwell. Finished, again, with the blemish-free plaster surface and painted satin titanium white, the light bouncing off the plaster surfaces of the recess is thrown in a steep wedge to fill only three quarters of the chamber with reflected light, leaving the enclosure's Yugoslavian Sivec marble surfaces—whose character is lost when lighted—in shadow. The warmer 3,000-degree-Kelvin color temperature of the lamps accentuates the warmer tones of stair's limestone treads and highlights its nick-el silver rails, which cascade through the volume like sparkling ribbons. A glass partition was used in place of an interior stair rail to permit the light to read through it shadow-free and minimize visual complexity.

The lamp life of the halogen sources used in the boutique is about 2,000 hours; for the fluorescents it is about 20,000. Because so much of the light is reflected, the lighting load for the entire space is approximately 12 watts/square foot, a bit above average for a high-end specialty boutique.

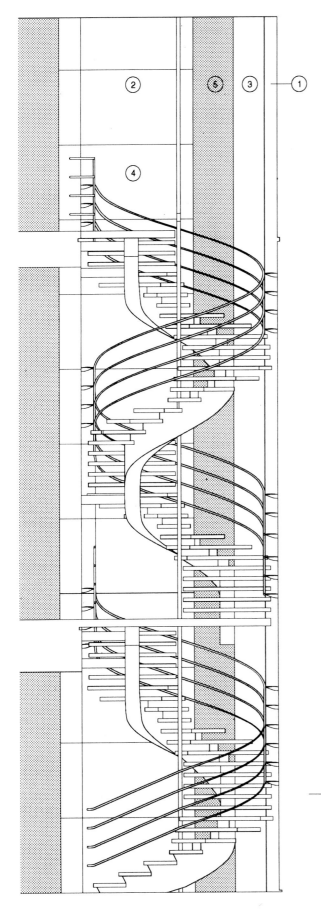

Stair Elevation w/ Vertical Light Slot

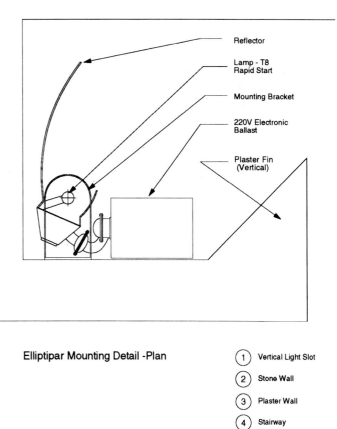

Reflector

Lamp - T8
Rapid Start

Mounting Bracket

220V Electronic
Ballast

Plaster Fin
(Vertical)

Elliptipar Mounting Detail -Plan

① Vertical Light Slot

② Stone Wall

③ Plaster Wall

④ Stairway

⑤ Open to Beyond

KENNETH COLE

Location: New York, New York

Architect: Edward I. Mills & Associates

Lighting Designer: Edward I. Mills & Associates

Manufacturers: McNichols Co. (metal mesh); Kern Rockenfield, Inc. (steel tubes, clips, brackets, and plates); Sylvania (MR-16s, PAR 38 quartz lamps).

Date Completed: November 1989

Photography: Peter Aaron/ESTO

In his design for the Kenneth Cole shoe store on Fifth Avenue in lower Manhattan, architect Edward I. Mills of Edward I. Mills & Associates has created a lighting element that accomplishes several illumination objectives, while piquantly complementing the bold earthiness of the interior architecture.

A construction of exposed lamps, bowed steel armatures, and a haphazardly unfurled band of metal mesh, this element is the store's predominant lighting feature. It creates a jagged, accordionlike screen across the 18-foot-high ceiling while meshing with the irregular angles and curves of the interior architecture and animating the space with an organic repetition of form, line, and light. Likened by the architect to Bernini's colonnade in St. Peter's cathedral in Rome, the lighting element produces a spontaneous sparkle amidst the interior's otherwise muted finishes of rough concrete, wood, and patinaed bronze and steel. Though the sparkle is an intended side effect, the lighting element also plays more important roles in providing both general illumination and focused spotlighting on the merchandise placed on shelves below. It also serves the architectural purpose of concealing an exposed ceiling duct, which extends the length of the space, and an air-conditioning unit in the back of the space.

The mesh was cut on site to fit the space and adequately cover the elements that needed to be hidden. The armatures supporting both the mesh and lamps are constructed of 3/4-inch-diameter, arced steel tubes bolted to two steel plates cut to partially fill the open space between the tubes. A custom-designed

angled clip connects each armature to the mesh, and once the elements were positioned into place, the entire construction was stabilized with cable that zigzags from the armatures to brackets on the ceiling. Conduit runs along the bottom tubes supplying power to three downlights affixed to the armatures' undersides. Upon each armature, two line-voltage, 75-watt MR-16s are positioned beneath the mesh to provide focused spotlight toward the window displays, and a 150-watt PAR 38 quartz lamp is positioned at its tip to light the floor with enough illumination to prevent an abundance of shadows.

The placement of the fixture was significant not only as an architectural screen for the ductwork, but to limit glare. Though indirect light would have been preferable, according to the architect the nature of the space and interior configuration didn't allow for it. By positioning the light high above the head, the potential for direct glare is diminished from within and from outside, where it is visible through floor-to-ceiling mullioned window walls.

The light from this element is also complemented by additional MR-16s on the ceiling, halogen wall washers, and tungsten light beneath the shelving. Though the sources demand a higher average lighting load of 7-8 watts/foot, and their lamp life is 3,000 hours, they were selected for their color rendering capability in this setting. The combined effect of their beam spreads was also considered essential in that the MR-16s offer focused spotlight on the shoes while the reflected brightness of the quartz lamps emphasized the architectural surfaces and minimized shadows around the shoes.

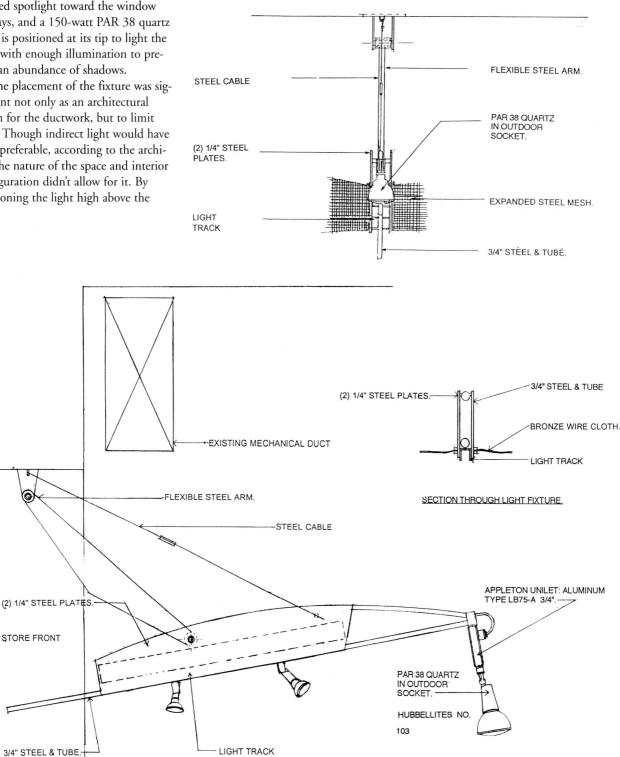

STEEL CABLE

(2) 1/4" STEEL PLATES.

LIGHT TRACK

FLEXIBLE STEEL ARM.

PAR 38 QUARTZ IN OUTDOOR SOCKET.

EXPANDED STEEL MESH.

3/4" STEEL & TUBE.

(2) 1/4" STEEL PLATES.

3/4" STEEL & TUBE

BRONZE WIRE CLOTH.

LIGHT TRACK

SECTION THROUGH LIGHT FIXTURE.

EXISTING MECHANICAL DUCT

FLEXIBLE STEEL ARM.

STEEL CABLE

(2) 1/4" STEEL PLATES.

STORE FRONT

APPLETON UNILET: ALUMINUM TYPE LB75-A 3/4".

PAR 38 QUARTZ IN OUTDOOR SOCKET.

HUBBELLITES NO. 103

3/4" STEEL & TUBE.

LIGHT TRACK

159

MATSUYA

Location: Fukuoka, Japan
Interior Designer: Yabu Pushelberg
Lighting Designer: Yabu Pushelberg
Date Completed: April 1993
Photography: Takeshi Nacasa/Nacasa & Partners

To distinguish the main floor of the Matsuya department store from the many other retail operations in the large metropolis of Fukuoka, Japan, interior designers Yabu Pushelberg created a homelike environment with natural materials and biomorphic forms. Unlike the planning of most western retail settings—where different departments are defined with materials and colors that give them distinct identities—the departments in Matsuya flow into one another, connected by meandering serpentine paths and distinguished only by differing levels of light. Because of the store's heavy traffic, the designers focused their attention on the entrance's ceiling plane, into which an expressive lighting element is recessed.

The entrance is located on the building's corner and the lighting feature, a donut-shaped ring around a large structural column, draws the customer's eye toward the ceiling. Designed to take the place of a chandelier, the 17½-foot-diameter recessed ring of light also gives the illusion of height in the relatively low-ceilinged 9-foot-high space.

The lighting element is actually composed of two concentric lighted recessed rings. The primary recess is a 1-foot-deep-by-2½-foot-wide circular band containing 20 plaster-surfaced drums, each punctuated by a 50-watt MR-16 downlight in its center. Staggered compact fluorescents concealed within coves on either side of this recessed ring provide a uniform glow around the lighted drums, whose cylindrical forms echo the shape of the ring and rhythmically articulate it. The cool light around the coves—reflected off the interior surfaces of the recess, which are painted a fresh spring green—contrasts with the spots of the white light of the MR-16s, which are capped by egg-shaped frosted glass covers.

The other recessed ring is directly adjacent to the column, which is covered with bronze and blue-green handmade glass tiles. Eight 50-watt MR-16 downlights are mounted within the recess and cast uneven light on the surface of the column, emphasizing the rippled imperfections of the tiles. In addition, five more MR-16s are recessed in the ceiling plane between the two rings to provide focused light on poster announcements or displays placed on a small table in front of the column. The low-voltage sources were chosen for their energy efficiency, compact size, color temperature, and high lumen output.

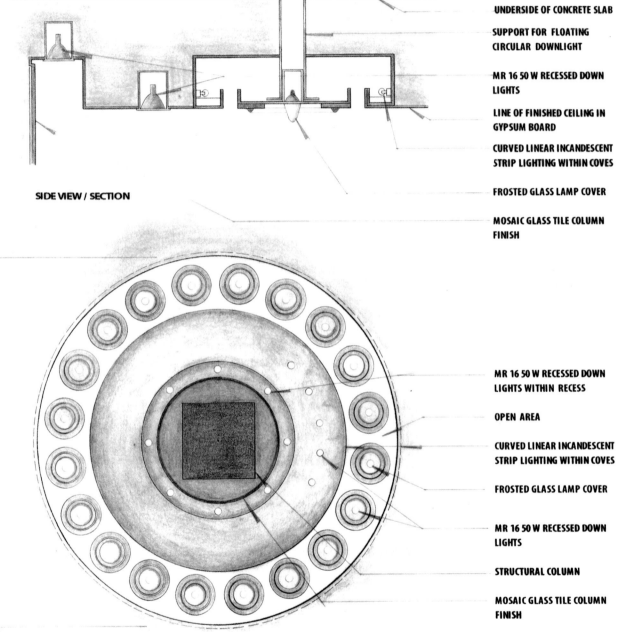

UNDERSIDE OF CONCRETE SLAB

SUPPORT FOR FLOATING
CIRCULAR DOWNLIGHT

MR 16 50 W RECESSED DOWN
LIGHTS

LINE OF FINISHED CEILING IN
GYPSUM BOARD

CURVED LINEAR INCANDESCENT
STRIP LIGHTING WITHIN COVES

FROSTED GLASS LAMP COVER

MOSAIC GLASS TILE COLUMN
FINISH

SIDE VIEW / SECTION

5400mm Ø

MR 16 50 W RECESSED DOWN
LIGHTS WITHIN RECESS

OPEN AREA

CURVED LINEAR INCANDESCENT
STRIP LIGHTING WITHIN COVES

FROSTED GLASS LAMP COVER

MR 16 50 W RECESSED DOWN
LIGHTS

STRUCTURAL COLUMN

MOSAIC GLASS TILE COLUMN
FINISH

REFLECTED PLAN VIEW

THEATER

DILLINGHAM HALL, PUNAHOU SCHOOL

Location: Honolulu, Oahu

Interior Architect: Hardy Holzman Pfeiffer Associates

Lighting Designer: Cline Bettridge Bernstein Lighting Design

Manufacturers: Arches: Mutual Welding Co. (steel arches); Duralite (A21 silver crown lamps). Stanchions: Mutual Welding Co. (metalwork, stanchions, grills globes); Sylvania (A99 lamps); Electronic Theater Controls (dimming system).

Date Completed: August 1994

Photography: David Franzen

Detail One: Arch Lights

Because its theater and music departments are among the most sophisticated in the nation, Honolulu's Punahou School, the largest independent prep school in the United States, commissioned Hardy Holzman Pfeiffer Associates to undertake an $8 million renovation of its theater in Dillingham Hall. Originally designed by Bertram Grovesnor Goodhue in 1929, the theater was remarkably minimalist, and unlike Goodhue's other highly decorated buildings, almost devoid of ornamentation

except for a series of structural concrete parabolic arches. In addition to modifying the theater to fulfill its current functional requirements, the architects added contemporary layers of ornamentation to bring vibrancy and vitality to Goodhue's original design without conflicting with its spirit. Two of the more significant ornamental additions, developed in conjunction with lighting designers Cline Bettridge Bernstein Lighting Design, are enlivened with integrated light.

The most dominant of these new additions are three pairs of new steel

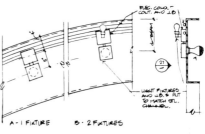

LIGHT FIXTURES @ STEEL ARCH.

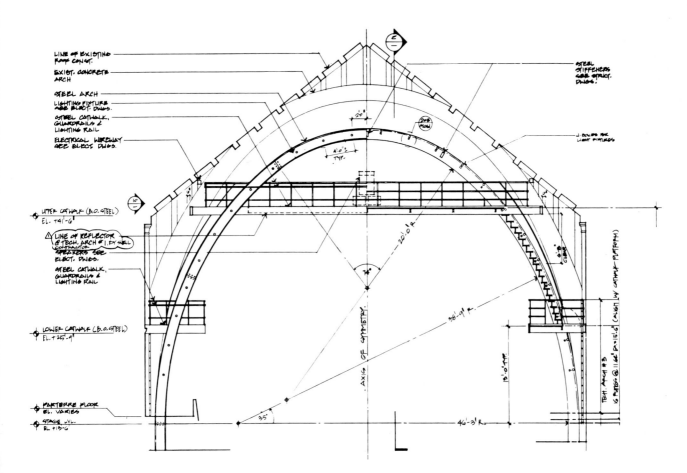

Dillingham Hall, Punahou School

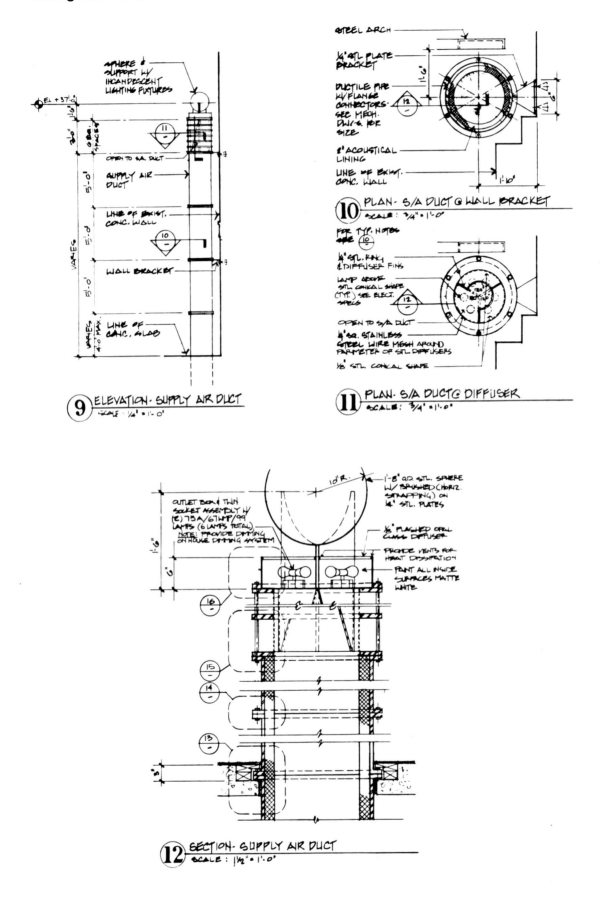

⑨ ELEVATION· SUPPLY AIR DUCT
SCALE : ¼" = 1'-0"

⑩ PLAN· S/A DUCT @ WALL BRACKET
SCALE : ¾" = 1'-0"

⑪ PLAN· S/A DUCT @ DIFFUSER
SCALE : ¾" = 1'-0"

⑫ SECTION· SUPPLY AIR DUCT
SCALE : 1½" = 1'-0"

parabolic arches that follow the shape of the concrete originals and support newly added catwalks for house lights, technical lighting, sound systems, and other production equipment. The architects distinguished the theater's new architectural features with a cool color palette that contrasts with the off-white color of the original elements. Painted a deep blue, the new arches are also punctuated with two kinds of low-wattage incandescent lamps, further distinguishing them from the originals while accentuating the theater's volume and animating it with sparkling light.

For decorative effect, each of the arches was custom-fabricated to accommodate 24 40-watt A21 silver crown lamps. Regularly positioned around the arches—three of which face the proscenium and three of which face the back of the theater—the lamps are mounted to junction boxes on their insides so they can be accessed from the catwalk. The lamps' filaments sparkle through their clear sides while the silver faces control glare. A second set of 30-watt R20 lamps, semi-recessed in porcelain sockets connected to spring-tempered steel mounting clips atop the junction boxes, distribute soft uplight on the ceiling and further accentuate the shape of the arches with a coronalike glow.

Detail Two: Stanchions

The original theater in Punahou's Dillingham Hall was designed without the benefit of modern ventilation systems. In order to bring it mechanically up to date and at once preserve the shape of the room, the architects developed 14 custom-designed vertical air supply stanchions which they placed in pairs around the space and ornamented by painting them a tropical green and illuminating their tops with concealed uplight.

Created in conjunction with lighting designers Cline Bettridge Bernstein, each 26-foot-high cylindrical stanchion is composed of standard 30-inch-diameter pipe with grillwork at the top and capped with a steel globe. To call attention to the stanchions and highlight the steel globes, six 75-watt A99 lamps concealed within a narrow coved collar above the grillwork illuminate the base

of the spheres with a soft halo of uplight. The lamps are positioned in twin socket assemblies mounted between each of the three flanges supporting the globe. To allow for an even distribution of light around the base of the globe, the lighting designers chose the largest light sources that would fit in the 6-inch-deep cove and covered it with an 1/8-inch-thick flashed opal glass diffuser. Semicircular cutouts at the edge of the glass allow for ventilation. The lighting designers also recommended that the

globes be manufactured of steel with vertical strapping to reflect and catch as much light as possible. In addition to highlighting the spheres atop the stanchions, the lamps slightly wash the walls and add another level of ambient illumination within the vast space.

To allow for control of the light level in the auditorium, both the lamps within the stanchions and those articulating the new parabolic arches are on individual circuits and connected to the house dimming system.

THE ED SULLIVAN THEATER

Location: New York, New York

Architect: Polshek and Partners

Lighting Designer: Fisher Marantz Renfro Stone

Date Completed: May 1994

Photography: Isaiah Wyner

When CBS took over Broadway's landmark Ed Sullivan Theater for "The Late Show with David Letterman," it turned to James Stewart Polshek and Partners, whose experience with historic structures as well as theater technology and design was vital to the project. Though the building's "gothic" detailing had been badly damaged over time, the Landmarks Preservation Commission's guidelines require that any alterations made to the original fabric of a landmarked structure for technical reasons be reversible. Converting the theater from a live performance space into a technically sophisticated broadcast studio meant reducing the size of the auditorium and introducing hundreds of lights, speakers, monitors, cableways, and other production paraphernalia. To respond to historic concerns while accommodating advanced technology and creating a more intimate space with refined acoustics, the architects developed two principal design interventions—the "sails" and the "ellipse"—which are defining features of the new set design within the existing theater.

Positioned on the balcony, the "sails" are gigantic concave acoustical membranes, resembling the cusplike forms of the Sydney Opera House. Aside from their acoustical function, they reduce the number of seats in the auditorium from 1,200 to 400. The "ellipse" is a lighted ceiling element, developed in conjunction with lighting designers Fisher Marantz Renfro Stone to reinforce the curvilinear geometry of the theater and unify the multiplicity of elements suspended from the ceiling—including stage lights, acoustical baffles, and extensive air conditioning ducts required to counteract the extreme heat generated by the lights.

Since cost was a major concern, the dimmable ellipse is an inexpensive but compelling design feature. It is simply composed of a series of molded aluminum U channels of various lengths, each with a wire raceway on top and two 51-watt traffic signal lamps mounted inside. Fastened end-to-end by metal tabs, the channels form an ellipse which is suspended by threaded rods to a steel-pipe support grid beneath the ceiling plane. To create the appearance of a continuous glow of light around the ellipse, the interior surface of each U channel was painted white to diffuse the light, while the silver-banded frosted lamps emit bursts of sparkle without glare. To keep the aluminum ellipse from "oil-canning," the base of the sides of each channel was bent inward for structural strength.

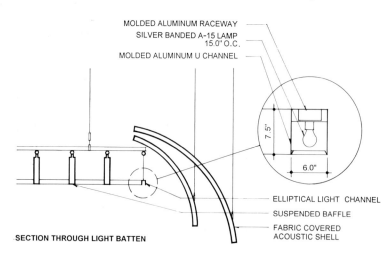

MOLDED ALUMINUM RACEWAY
SILVER BANDED A-15 LAMP
15.0" O.C.
MOLDED ALUMINUM U CHANNEL

7.5"

6.0"

ELLIPTICAL LIGHT CHANNEL
SUSPENDED BAFFLE
FABRIC COVERED ACOUSTIC SHELL

SECTION THROUGH LIGHT BATTEN

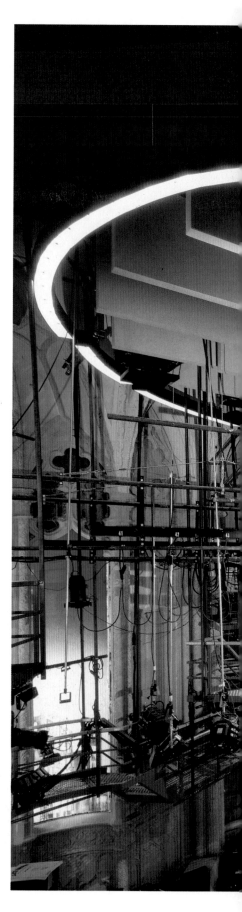

THE PRINCESS OF WALES THEATER

Location: Toronto, Ontario, Canada

Architect: Lett Smith Architects

Interior Designer: Yabu Pushelberg

Lighting Designer: Yabu Pushelberg

Manufacturers: Entrance foyer ceiling vault lighting: Norbert Belfer (incandescent strip); Targetti, Systema Luce (MR-16s); Moss+Lam (fin). Recessed star downlight: Formglass (fiberglass inset); Eureka (AR 48 reflector). Bar top fixture: Pancor Industry (contractor); Jeff Goodman (blown glass); V.N. Custom Metal (stainless-steel shade, chain skirt, and base). Hour glass sconce: Jeff Goodman (blown glass); V.N. Custom Metal (metal components). Newel Post: Jeff Goodman (blown glass); V.N. Custom Metal (metal components); Pancor Industry (mahogany post). Stairwell sconce: V.N. Custom Metal (metal components).

Date Completed: April 1993

Photography: Robert Burley/Design Archives; Evan Dion

Detail One: Entrance Foyer Coves and Spots

Unlike Toronto's mostly lusterless, institutional theater buildings, its Princess of Wales theater is lively, witty, and voluptuous. In response to the owner's request for a space that would draw people in, regardless of what might be on stage, interior designers Yabu Pushelberg created lush, sensuous spaces that evoke the glitter of night with bold exotic forms, rich texture, and lavish color. Taking as their models the classic opera houses of the 19th century, the designers infused the theater with traditional rich finishes and luxurious detailing, yet did so with an utterly fresh point of view. While the attention to detailing is seen throughout, the delightful handling of lighting—both as architecturally integrated elements and in several whimsical and exquisitely crafted custom fixtures—particularly enliven the spectacle.

The first of these lighting elements accentuates the dazzling entry foyer, a long corridor lined with oversize gold-painted columns along either side of a vaulted ceiling, which is finished with mosaic tiles, gold and silver leaf, and patterned with star-studded diamond shapes. Since the theater is shoehorned into a tight space and the foyer is located beneath the auditorium in a low-ceilinged space, the designers used light to create the illusion of a more expansive volume, heightening the appearance of the ceiling with glowing light. Linear incandescent strip lighting hidden within undulating coves on either side of the vault accentuate their curves and highlight the vault with continuous bands of warm light, while recessed MR-16 spot downlights help articulate the ceiling pattern, pop up the floor, and lend sparkle.

Since the foyer is filled with people before performances and during intermissions, the designers focused on the ceiling, detailing it with luminous, reflective materials that promote an atmosphere of entertainment and celebration. They also wanted to make sure that patrons looked good, so the warmer incandescent strip lights—whose lamps abut one another to appear as a band of continuous light and provide the primary illumination in this space—not only lift the ceiling and call attention to its detailing but pleasingly render the patrons' skin tones with warm reflected shadowless light. The coves are hand painted with a white finish and lined with glass tiles to reflect scintillating light. The narrow 27-degree beams of the compact MR-16s positioned at the intersections of the diamond patterns on the ceiling are aimed toward the walls to minimize shadows. Those in the star points along the center of the vault are fitted with glass trims that reflect and spread the light around the edges of the lamps, thereby highlighting the mosaic.

Complementing the light in and along the vault are charming wall sconces that evoke the tasseled fringe of a theater curtain. The sconces contribute to the overall lighting scheme for this space by offering punctuated points of diffused, shimmering light along the walls on either side of the space. Simply executed with skirts of chain mail in front of incandescent sources affixed to the wall, the sconces are clever glittering accents.

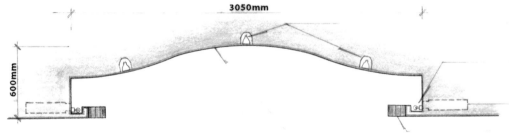

3050mm

600mm

MR 16 50 W RECESSED DOWN
LIGHTS

LINEAR INCANDESCENT STRIP
LIGHTING WITHIN COVE

AIR SUPPLY

UNDULATING COVE EDGE

PLASTER FINISH CURVED
GYPSUM BOARD

SECTION VIEW

MAIN HALL SECTION VIEW

The Princess of Wales Theater

Detail Three: Bar Fixtures

Complementing the ceiling lighting in the lounge of the Princess of Wales theater are two other custom fixtures which call attention to the three bars. One is a sort of elongated mushroom-shaped fixture atop the bars, and the other is an hour-glass-shaped sconce on the wall behind each bar. Each is composed of blown glass and metal detailing, adding whimsy and sensuality to this heavily visited area during intermissions.

The design of the bar-top fixture was influenced by three essential objectives: that it serve as an ornamental beacon, that it be durable, and that its profile be slender enough to allow beverages to be passed over the bar without hindrance. In response to these concerns, the designers created sleek shafts of resilient blown glass capped with spun stainless-steel reflectors and stainless-steel bases, and mounted them on the Atlantic black granite bar-top surface, which was honed to prevent reflected glare.

Each of the narrow 18-inch-high fixtures is fitted with 35-watt quartz halogen MR-11 lamps. Mounted beneath the bar top, the sources were chosen for their high luminance, compact size, and narrow beams which pass concentrated, intense direct light through the green glass shafts. The light is diffused through the tiny air bubbles of the glass and directed toward the stainless-steel dome, which reflects it back down toward the chain mail skirt, eliciting a shimmering sparkle. Fed by a remote transformer located within the cabinetry

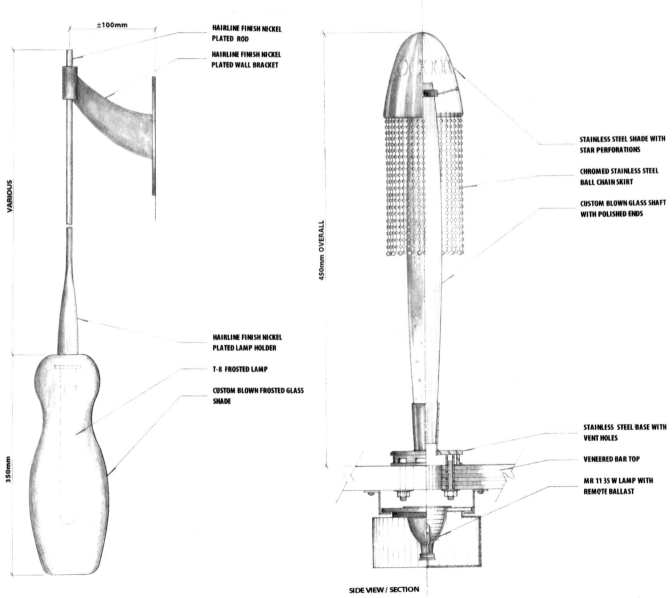

±100mm

HAIRLINE FINISH NICKEL PLATED ROD

HAIRLINE FINISH NICKEL PLATED WALL BRACKET

VARIOUS

HAIRLINE FINISH NICKEL PLATED LAMP HOLDER

T-8 FROSTED LAMP

CUSTOM BLOWN FROSTED GLASS SHADE

350mm

SIDE VIEW

STAINLESS STEEL SHADE WITH STAR PERFORATIONS

CHROMED STAINLESS STEEL BALL CHAIN SKIRT

CUSTOM BLOWN GLASS SHAFT WITH POLISHED ENDS

450mm OVERALL

STAINLESS STEEL BASE WITH VENT HOLES

VENEERED BAR TOP

MR 11 35 W LAMP WITH REMOTE BALLAST

SIDE VIEW / SECTION

BAR FIXTURE

of the bar, radiant heat from these sources is conveniently deflected through their backs.

The sinuous curves of the hourglass-shaped sconces behind the bar echo the hourglass timers on the bars which tell patrons how much time they have before intermission ends. Their vertical profile also corresponds to the elongated bar-top fixtures.

Each fixture is composed of a 14-inch-high, frosted hand-blown glass shade suspended from the wall by hair-line-finished nickel-plated stems. To evenly illuminate the length of the fix-ture's vertical profile with warm light, the designers used frosted tubular 60-watt T-18 incandescents designed for aquariums. Through the snow-white glass their yellow light is softened to cre-ate a warm pleasing glow.

The Princess of Wales Theater

Detail Four:
Chain Sconce and Baluster

Two other lighting elements contribute to the lively mix of custom light fixtures in the Princess of Wales theater. Though very different in their construction, both features were designed to call attention to the stairs. One of them takes the form of an orb-shaped finial atop a newel post positioned in front of each of the two main stairways on either end of the foyer. The other is a series of wall sconces illuminating the stairways to the upper levels of the theater.

Since the theater was planned in the manner of 19th-century European opera houses, the entrances were placed on the sides of the theater rather than at the rear as is typical in North America. To ease any sense of disorientation that would come from the uncustomary plan, the newel baluster was designed to direct circulation toward the stairs by serving as a beacon. Each 54-inch-high fixture is constructed of a marble base, a non-threatened species of solid Honduran mahogany baluster, and a clear blown glass orb laced with a blue spiral which conceals the recessed 50-watt MR-16 lamp within at the top. The MR-16 was chosen first for its high light output level and lack of radiant heat. Its consistency with other lamps used throughout the space and relatively long life of 5,000 rated hours also eases maintenance.

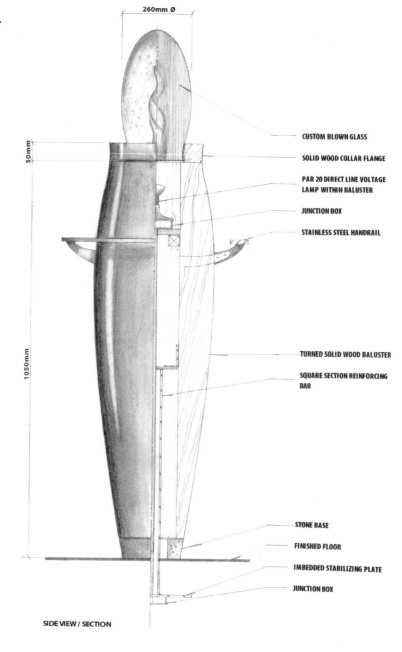

260mm Ø

50mm

1050mm

CUSTOM BLOWN GLASS

SOLID WOOD COLLAR FLANGE

PAR 20 DIRECT LINE VOLTAGE LAMP WITHIN BALUSTER

JUNCTION BOX

STAINLESS STEEL HANDRAIL

TURNED SOLID WOOD BALUSTER

SQUARE SECTION REINFORCING BAR

STONE BASE

FINISHED FLOOR

IMBEDDED STABILIZING PLATE

JUNCTION BOX

SIDE VIEW / SECTION

ILLUMINATED BALUSTER

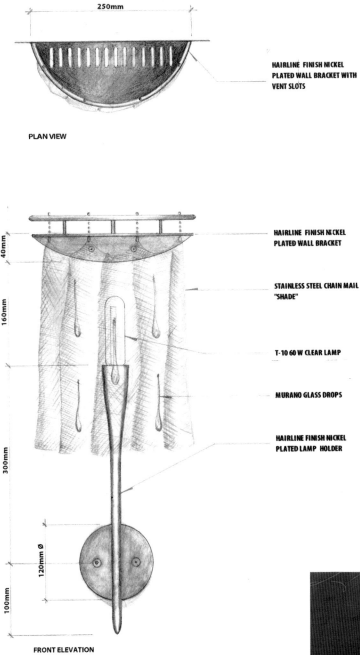

250mm

HAIRLINE FINISH NICKEL
PLATED WALL BRACKET WITH
VENT SLOTS

PLAN VIEW

40mm

HAIRLINE FINISH NICKEL
PLATED WALL BRACKET

160mm

STAINLESS STEEL CHAIN MAIL
"SHADE"

T-10 60 W CLEAR LAMP

MURANO GLASS DROPS

300mm

HAIRLINE FINISH NICKEL
PLATED LAMP HOLDER

120mm Ø

100mm

FRONT ELEVATION

WALL SCONCE

The wall sconces were designed to be the sole source of illumination in the secondary stairwells that connect the theater's various levels. The low ceilings and tight space constraints in these stairwells eliminated the possibility of mounting overhead fixtures. As a result, wall sconces were designed to project only 4 inches into the space. Mounted 6 feet above the floor, each sconce is composed simply of a chain mail skirt decorated with drops of handmade Murano glass, which is draped from a hairline finished nickel-plate bracket concealing a 100-watt halogen lamp mounted to the wall.

Because they are the only source of illumination in the stairwells, the halogen sources were chosen for their high lumen output, which passes upward through a slot in the bracket toward the ivory-colored plaster ceiling and through the chain mail skirts, creating decorative patterns on the walls. Their high color-rendering index was also an important factor in proper illumination of the plaster walls, which are richly striped in two tones of oxblood tint overlaid with gold hand-painted motifs.

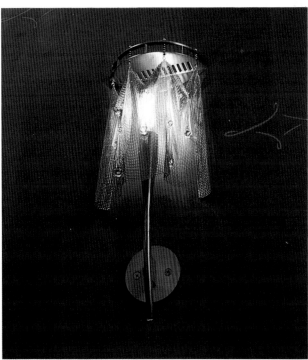

Shepard Hall Recital Hall, City College of the City University of New York

Location: New York, New York

Interior Designer: William A. Hall Partnership

Lighting Designer: Fisher Marantz Renfro Stone

Acoustic Consultants: Shen Milsom Wilke

Manufacturers: Quarter-turn fixture: Rohm & Haas (Plexiglas diffusers); Norbert Belfer (incandescent lamps). Suspended stage fixtures: Louis Baldinger & Sons.

Date Completed: October 1992

Photography: Wade Zimmerman

Detail One: Quarter-Turn Fixture

Originally designed by architect George B. Post in 1904, Shepard Hall is an historic building recently renovated by the William A. Hall Partnership on the campus of the City College of New York. In designing a new theater in the old mechanical area of Shepard Hall the architects went to great lengths to produce a space that would respect the traditional aesthetic of the landmark building. But acoustic and lighting concerns were also key in the development of the theater, which in addition functions as a classroom and lecture hall. Two architectural elements in the theater deftly respond to all three of the architects' objectives.

One of these elements, integrated with the maple millwork along the back wall of the theater, is a "quarter-turn" light fixture which doubles as an acoustical diffuser. Developed in conjunction with lighting designers Fisher Marantz Renfro Stone and acoustical consultants Shen Milsom Wilke, it was designed to provide accent light to the auditorium when it operates as a performance space. A separate fluorescent system, which includes warm-white compact sources hidden behind gigantic diffusing disks in the ceiling, raises the level of illumination to 40 to 50 footcandles when the space functions as a classroom.

Positioned in the 90-degree angle where the back wall meets the ceiling, the convex surface of the 2-foot-deep "quarter-turn" fixture reflects sound coming from the stage and prevents an untimely reverb. It is simply constructed of a series of vacuum-formed, 4-foot-wide, frosted Plexiglas lenses supported by a frame of wood struts extending from the millwork. Concealing a strip light containing 40-watt A19 lamps positioned 6 inches on center and surface-mounted along the back wall within each bay of the fixture, the 1/4-inch-thick lenses are 47 percent transmissive and have a P80 matte finish on the outside. They simply lift out for access to the lamps. The lamps in the fixture are on a separate dimming channel for individual control.

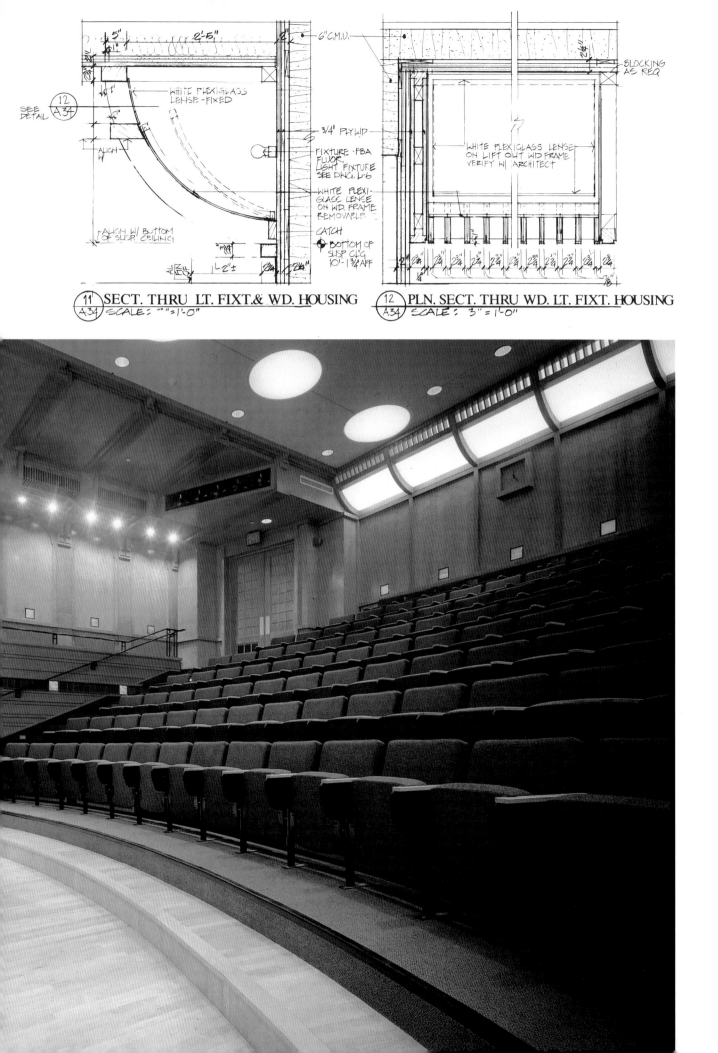

11 / A34 SECT. THRU LT. FIXT. & WD. HOUSING SCALE: ?"=1'-0"

12 / A34 PLN. SECT. THRU WD. LT. FIXT. HOUSING SCALE: 3"=1'-0"

Shepard Hall Recital Hall

Detail Two: Umbrella Pendants

Also part of the incandescent system and designed as acoustical reflectors-cum-light sources are three umbrellalike fixtures suspended over the stage of the Shepard Hall theater. Though few luminaires or historic documents were found for reference during the renovation, original hemispheric pendants in the building's corridors inspired the shapes of the fixtures above the stage. The use of both fluorescent and incandescent systems allowed the space to meet state energy codes. To remain true to the warmer gaslighting originally used in the building, the umbrella fixtures in this space incorporate low-wattage incandescent sources. Like the quarter-turn fixture, their convex forms are ideally suited to reflect sound, in this case both vertically and horizontally. They offer diffuse light directly on the stage and include a direct downlight in the center for focused stage lighting.

To fulfill both their lighting and acoustical functions, the scale of the fixtures is large—the central fixture is 9 feet in diameter and the two flanking fixtures are each 6 feet. They are composed of a series of 1/4-inch-thick translucent white acrylic diffuser panels fitted within an umbrellalike aluminum armature and suspended from the ceiling by a series of rigid rods. To recall the building's original wrought-iron metalwork, the armature has a dark painted finish, and the rods are capped with decorative spun aluminum coverplates at the ceiling. Wiring threaded through a central hollow rod feeds power to the 40-watt A lamps contained in each of the umbrellalike diffusers. Mounted to horizontal rigid rods projecting from the central vertical rod, the lamps are composed in a layered radial pattern to evenly distribute ample light throughout the fixtures. Supplementing the recessed ceiling downlights, a recessed 250-watt PAR 38 quartz lamp in the center of each fixture casts focused direct downlight on the stage. It is fitted with a low-brightness reflector cone to shield the lamp and prevent glare when viewed from the audience.

Like the quarter-turn fixture, the fixtures' acrylic diffusers have a matte P80 finish on one side to keep them from being specular. All of the fixtures are also connected to a dimming system.

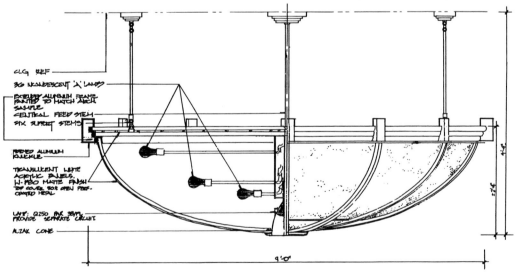

PARTIAL SECTION ELEVATION (FAV)
SCALE: 1 ½" = 1'-0"

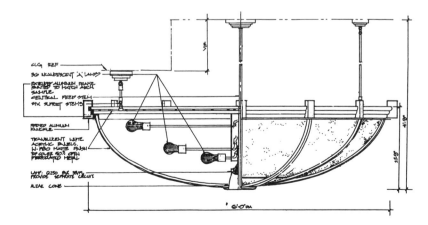

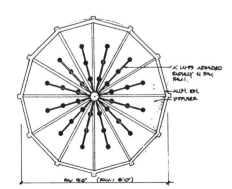

PARTIAL SECTION ELEVATION (FAV-1)
SCALE: 1½" = 1'-0"

TOP PLAN VIEW
SCALE: ½" = 1'-0"

SONY ENTERTAINMENT HEADQUARTERS

Location: New York, New York

Architect: Gwathmey Siegel Architects & Associates

Lighting Designer: Flack+Kurtz

Manufacturers: Starfire Xenflex (xenon strip lights); Cole Lighting (step light); Edison Price MR-16s).

Date Completed: June 1993

Photography: Durston Saylor

In Gwathmey Siegel Architects & Associates' renovation of Philip Johnson & John Burgee's former AT&T building for Sony Entertainment, one of the highest priority spaces was the seventh-floor screening room. Since visiting executives, celebrities, and test audiences view rough cuts, presentations, and private movie screenings in this space, both sophisticated design and attention to acoustics were of utmost importance. The architectural elements, in fact, are organized to defer to the acoustical demands. The task for lighting designers Flack+Kurtz was to integrate subtle low-key lighting elements that would heighten the strict lines of the architecture without calling attention to themselves.

Dictated by the primary emphasis on acoustics, the ceiling, for instance, is

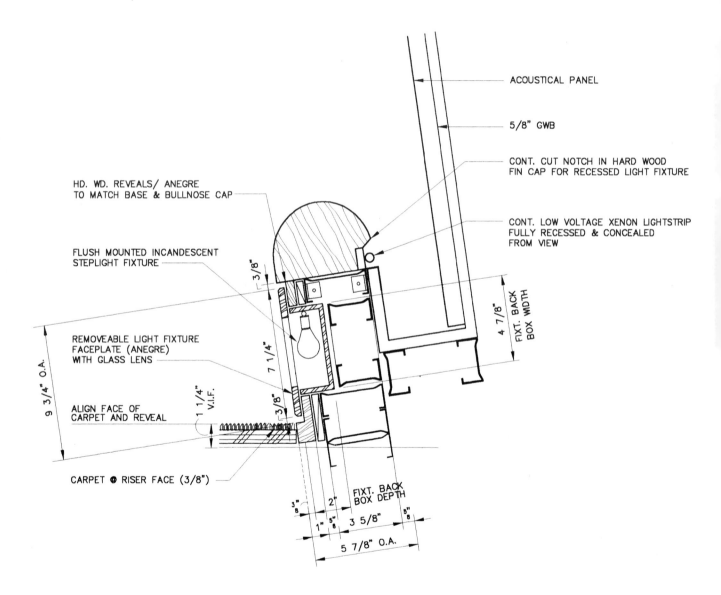

ACOUSTICAL PANEL

5/8" GWB

CONT. CUT NOTCH IN HARD WOOD FIN CAP FOR RECESSED LIGHT FIXTURE

CONT. LOW VOLTAGE XENON LIGHTSTRIP FULLY RECESSED & CONCEALED FROM VIEW

HD. WD. REVEALS/ ANEGRE TO MATCH BASE & BULLNOSE CAP

FLUSH MOUNTED INCANDESCENT STEPLIGHT FIXTURE

REMOVEABLE LIGHT FIXTURE FACEPLATE (ANEGRE) WITH GLASS LENS

ALIGN FACE OF CARPET AND REVEAL

CARPET ⊕ RISER FACE (3/8")

3/8"

7 1/4"

9 3/4" O.A.

1 1/4" V.I.F.

3/8"

4 7/8" FIXT. BACK BOX WIDTH

3" 8

2"

FIXT. BACK BOX DEPTH

1" 5" 8

3 5/8"

5" 8

5 7/8" O.A.

PLAN DETAIL AT FOOT LIGHT
SCALE: 3" = 1'-0"

organized into alternating strips of broad wood slats, which are resonant, and narrow gypsum board bands, which serve as sound attenuation bands. So as to preserve the integrity of the linear organization established by the ceiling elements, the lighting designers were limited to containing the downlights within 1-foot-wide gyp board bands, above which all of the sprinkler and fire alarm systems are also located. Compact MR-16s were used in the gyp-board bands as downlights on the seating, and because an additional acoustical ceiling above prevents heat from ventilating into the plenum, an air return duct was also sandwiched in. The horizontal lines of the ceiling were also carried into vertical architectural elements, again dictated by acoustical concerns. A series of angled, fabric-wrapped acoustical wall

panels are aligned between the gyp-board bands of the ceiling, and integrated, indirect light sources behind the panels provide a functional and aesthetic integration of light with architecture.

Running along the interior edge of the acoustical panels a low-voltage strip of 5-watt xenon strip lights was concealed in notches cut into anigre bull-nose endcaps, matching the wood of the ceiling slats. Instead of obstructing the clean lines of the architecture with decorative fixtures, or flattening the vertical surfaces with wall washers, the lighting designers' use of the concealed strip enhances the staggered vertical lines along the wall by evenly lighting them from top to bottom. They also serve the functional purpose of providing rhythmic illumination along the stair, while a standard 6-watt step light, concealed in

a pocket and covered with a glass face plate at the base of each panel, serves as a safety light which illuminates the steps when the primary lighting is dimmed.

Each lamp in the low-voltage strip is positioned 3 inches on center at a one-to-one ratio from the surface off which it reflects, thereby creating the effect of continuous illumination along the edges of the panels. Xenon lamps were chosen because their small size would interfere least with the lines of the architecture. In addition, they offer the required low level of illumination, and their color temperature of 2,800 degrees Kelvin closely matches the dimmed MR-16 downlights in the ceiling. A neutral beige fabric was chosen to cover the panels and complement the warm light. The lamps are connected to a remote dimming transformer.

Detail Two:
Entry Hallway Trough

The other light trough in the Goldberg Bean house appears along the windowed entry hallway facing the city and ocean. While the concept and the light source are the same, the execution is entirely different, as were the programmatic demands. Here, sufficient illumination was required to see down the 30-foot-long hallway at night, but the light level needed to be low enough so that it wouldn't reflect off the glass windows and block the view of the landscape, Century City lights, and ocean beyond.

The architect's response was to lay the light source on a stainless-steel shelf, which is located above the windows and extends in two sections along the entire length of the hall. The sheets of 1/8-inch-thick brushed stainless steel were mounted to the 1/2-inch-thick plywood framing above the windows with counter sunk stainless steel screws. The brushed steel panels extend 6 inches into the hallway and are bent at a 20-degree angle toward the ceiling to conceal the light source.

The brushed stainless-steel surfaces, which increase the reflection of the light, are divided by and visually linked with an interior metallic-painted steel structural column, which was added to support the cantilevered porch. The ends of each shelf are capped with infill panels to completely conceal the light source from view.

The non-neon light sources in both the hall shelf and the living room wall cove are advantageous both in terms of cost and from a mechanical standpoint. At $8 per linear foot they are substantially lower in price than most low-voltage light sources, and at 110-volts, did not require the installation of a tranformer. In addition, while most line-voltage sources require a power feed every 7 to 10 feet, at 110 volts the non-neon tube light can run up to 120 feet from a single connection. Here they were cut on site and connected directly into the electrical system.

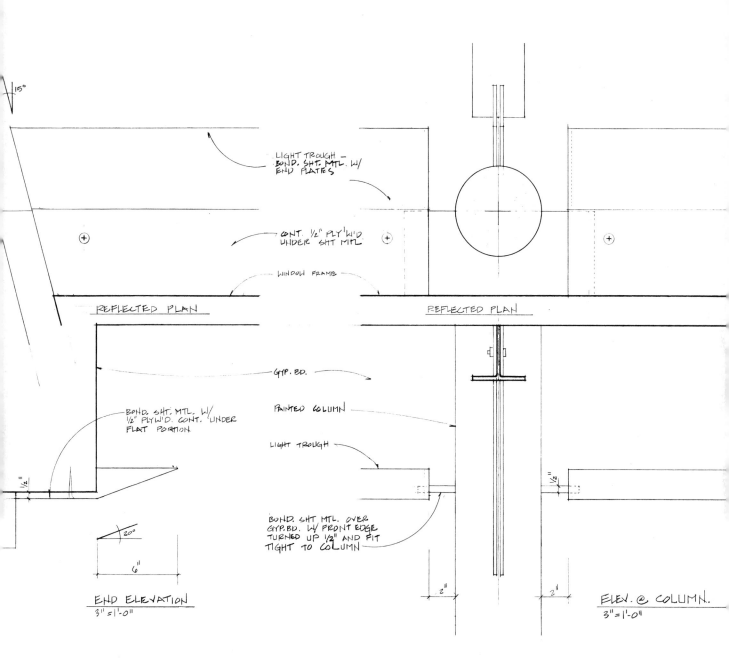

15°

LIGHT TROUGH —
BOND. SHT. MTL. W/
END PLATES

CONT. ½" PLY'WD.
UNDER SHT MTL.

WINDOW FRAME

REFLECTED PLAN

REFLECTED PLAN

GYP. BD.

BOND. SHT. MTL. W/
½" PLY'WD. CONT. UNDER
FLAT PORTION.

PAINTED COLUMN

LIGHT TROUGH

½"

½"

BOND. SHT MTL. OVER
GYP. BD. W/ FRONT EDGE
TURNED UP ½" AND FIT
TIGHT TO COLUMN

20°

6"

2"

2"

END ELEVATION
3" = 1'-0"

ELEV. @ COLUMN.
3" = 1'-0"

Lawson Westen Residence

Location: Los Angeles, California

Architect: Eric Owen Moss, Architect

Lighting Designer: Saul Golden

Fabricators: Philips (compact fluorescent); Sylvania (Designer 16 PAR lamps); Stonco (Lexan Globe corrugated cover); Crouse-Hinds (sockets and other electrical components).

Date Completed: March 1993

Photography: Tom Bonner

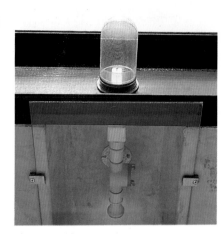

Given his predisposition for creating architecture that is as enigmatic as it is compelling, it is not surprising that architect Eric Owen Moss's design for the Lawson Westen residence in West Los Angeles overturns traditional notions associated with home. The heart of the structure, a four-story kitchen topped with an off-center roof cone, confounds immediate understanding: Intonations of typically obscure spaces—the attic and basement—are brought into plain view and melded into the expression of this central space. The owners requested eccentric lighting, so the designer used a series of custom fixtures, notably an exterior fixture integrated within the soffit above its front door.

The exterior fixtures are composites of standard pieces put together in a non-standard fashion and tied to the structure. In the plaster soffit above the passage leading to the door, five 9-inch-deep coffered slots are fitted with alternating configurations of compact fluorescent and miniature Designer 16 PAR spot sources. The lamps are connected to a central socket suspended from the ceiling plane by a short steel-pipe coupling, and the slots are partially covered with plates of laminated glass to shield the fixtures from dirt and moisture. They are held in place by custom steel clips, which are bolted to the ceiling surface and can be easily removed for maintenance. Protruding from the steel beam, a corrugated cover, which was partially cut to reveal the tip of the lamp, nominally protects the lamp from the elements.

The collection of lighted slots seem to change according to the vantage point, whether the lights are on or off. The architect was as interested in expressing the lighting elements as objects in and of themselves as he was in how well they illuminated the surrounding surfaces. Because of the distinct natures of the different lamps and their irregular configurations, light is distributed asymmetrically in opposite directions, reflected off the interior wall and ceiling surfaces, and directed toward the ground.

While the lamps were selected for their inherent sculptural qualities and combined in a manner that accentuates them, the cooler fluorescents and good color rendering capabilities of the 55-watt PAR lamps also bring out the subtleties in the blue, yellow, and gray coloration of the plaster surfaces.

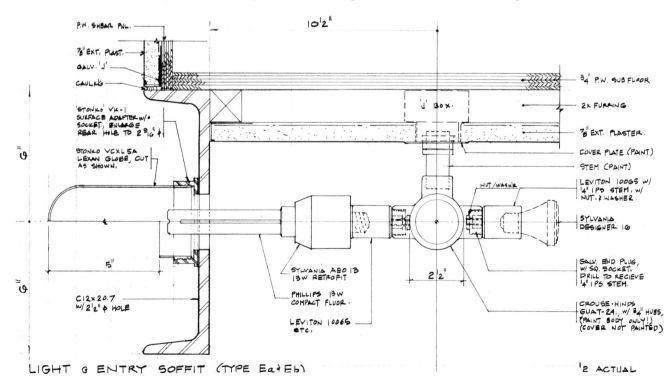

LIGHT @ ENTRY SOFFIT (TYPE Ea+Eb)   ½ ACTUAL

MAGRAM RESIDENCE

Location: New York, New York

Interior Designer: Neiman and Wood Interior Design

Lighting Designer: James Wood

Manufacturers: CJ Lighting/Lutron (electrical components); Passeri Marble (onyx panels); Metalworks, Inc. (stainless-steel frames).

Date Completed: February 1992

Photography: Derrick & Love

In keeping with the tastes of its corporate executive owner, a Manhattan penthouse apartment designed by Neiman and Wood is characterized by a modern aesthetic with crisp, clean lines and contemporary furnishings. In order to maintain the purity of the spare design yet infuse the space with a warm, residential quality, the designers used simple, clean architectural forms with subtle finishes and interesting materials as decorative elements. A series of custom-designed light features in a long central hallway epitomize the designers' ingenuity in creating architectural solutions that are as visually enticing as they are functional.

Two separate adjoining apartments connected by a 75-foot-long hall comprise the residence, and the custom light elements punctuating the walls on either side of this hall not only illuminate its long expanse but add aesthetic variety both in terms of material and modulated light. The rooms on one side of the hall are lined with perimeter terraces and have windows that open to panoramic views. To allow the daylight to permeate through the rooms to the central hall, the designers made the rooms semi-transparent with full-height, folding sandblasted glass doors which open onto the hall. The custom light elements are positioned at eye level along the fabric-covered walls between the doors to increase the level of illumination along the hall. They also provide a warm light that contrasts with the daylight streaming through the doors.

The lighting features are actually recessed light pockets covered with panes of white onyx. Because the hall is

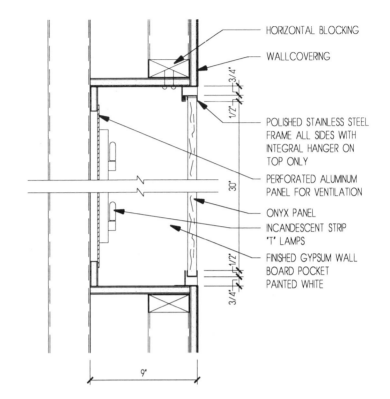

HORIZONTAL BLOCKING

WALLCOVERING

POLISHED STAINLESS STEEL FRAME ALL SIDES WITH INTEGRAL HANGER ON TOP ONLY

PERFORATED ALUMINUM PANEL FOR VENTILATION

ONYX PANEL

INCANDESCENT STRIP 'T' LAMPS

FINISHED GYPSUM WALL BOARD POCKET PAINTED WHITE

30"

3/4"

1/2"

1/2"

3/4"

9'

VERTICAL SECTION

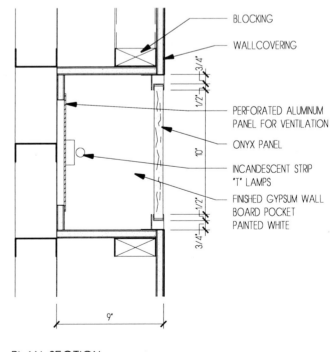

BLOCKING

WALLCOVERING

PERFORATED ALUMINUM PANEL FOR VENTILATION

ONYX PANEL

INCANDESCENT STRIP 'T' LAMPS

FINISHED GYPSUM WALL BOARD POCKET PAINTED WHITE

10"

3/4"

1/2"

1/2"

3/4"

9'

PLAN SECTION

narrow, the 30-inch-high-by-10-inch-wide onyx-panels facing the recesses were mounted flush with the walls. Each 9-inch-deep recess contains four 40-watt incandescent T-lamps mounted on a continuous strip socket. The lamps are surface-mounted to an aluminum panel, which is perforated to allow for ventilation, and the interior gypsum wall board surfaces of the recesses were painted white to increase reflectivity. Positioned vertically along the center of the recess, the lamps, though spaced 8 inches apart, appear to provide diffuse, continuous light through the 3/4-inch-thick onyx panels. To create balanced light levels, the lamps are on dimmers, allowing the light output to be higher during the day to compensate for the daylight and then dimmed at night.

Though the fixtures were specifically designed to give off a warm soft glow to complement the matte finishes on the surrounding surfaces, including the hand-waxed teak herringbone inlaid floor and fabric wallcovering, the designers also wanted the hall to exude a bit of sparkle. To create it, they framed the light fixtures with strips of cool, polished stainless steel, a sort of inverse echo of the Chinese red lacquer frames surrounding the sandblasted glass doors.

EXTERIOR

CENTER FOR THE ARTS THEATER AT YERBA BUENA GARDENS

Location: San Francisco, California

Architect: Polshek and Partners

Lighting Designer: Synergy Consultants

Manufacturers: Norbert Belfer (strip lights); Hydrel (recessed MR-16s); Infranor (metal halides); Toland Iron Works (aluminum screen and custom metal work).

Date Completed: October 1993

Photography: Richard Barnes/ESTO

Detail One: Recessed Plaza Lights

Without a significant context upon which to draw for their design of the Center for the Arts at San Francisco's newly formed Yerba Buena Gardens, architects Polshek and Partners relied instead on the city's multi-cultural arts community as a point of reference. One of the key elements in a bold urban design experiment undertaken by the city to revitalize one of its under-used districts with a complex of buildings dedicated to the performing arts, the theater is an assemblage of cubist volumes inspired by Far Eastern precedents. Designed to showcase local talent, its two primary forms—a dark grey cube housing the theater and a silver trapezoid containing the audience chamber—derive from the Japanese game of Go, while its additional volumes, rendered in black and white, harmoniously round out the composition with a balanced blend of yin and yang. Designed to be as striking at night as it is during the day, the structure's geometric volumes and planes are enhanced in the evening hours by the architect's inspired use of light.

Its main lobby, for instance, is a 36-foot cubic light box with a Chinese red marquis announcing the principal entry. A subtle treatment of the mandatory lighting features illuminating the outdoor plaza in front of the lobby allow the glass-faced cube to stand out as a glowing lantern. Developed in conjunc-tion with lighting designers Synergy Consultants, two lighting details embedded within the plaza floor punctuate the foreground with just enough light to accent important junctures.

Both of these details graciously enhance the procession toward the theater. The first is a recessed feature illuminating the steps leading up to the plaza with staccato dashes of warm light. Casting a path of reflected light on the risers, 3- and 4-foot-long strips of low-voltage xenon tungsten-halogen lamps, spaced 2 inches on center, are mounted to a steel angle cast in a recess on the underside of the concrete steps. The strip light—with its long life of 50,000 hours and 14-volt transformer remotely located beneath the plaza pavers—was chosen for its architectural effect, low cost, and ease of maintenance.

While the theater reads as a study in black and white during the day, at night its planes of primary color accentuated by the light are an integral part of the evening's physical and social sequence of events. Like a raised red carpet, the illuminated canopy initiates the passage toward the evening's event, with the light-washed yellow wall enclosing the back of the lobby heightening the anticipation of the drama about to unfold, and the calming blue walls of the theater soothing the atmosphere as the performance is about to begin.

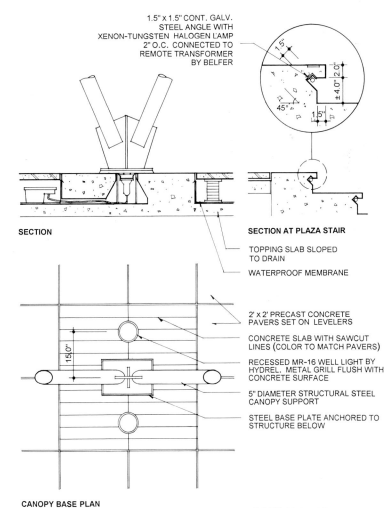

1.5" x 1.5" CONT. GALV. STEEL ANGLE WITH XENON-TUNGSTEN HALOGEN LAMP 2" O.C. CONNECTED TO REMOTE TRANSFORMER BY BELFER

SECTION

SECTION AT PLAZA STAIR

TOPPING SLAB SLOPED TO DRAIN

WATERPROOF MEMBRANE

2' x 2' PRECAST CONCRETE PAVERS SET ON LEVELERS

CONCRETE SLAB WITH SAWCUT LINES (COLOR TO MATCH PAVERS)

RECESSED MR-16 WELL LIGHT BY HYDREL. METAL GRILL FLUSH WITH CONCRETE SURFACE

5" DIAMETER STRUCTURAL STEEL CANOPY SUPPORT

STEEL BASE PLATE ANCHORED TO STRUCTURE BELOW

CANOPY BASE PLAN

©1995 Polshek and Partners, LLP

Center for the Arts Theater at Yerba Buena Gardens

The other exterior lighting detail, a recessed uplight illuminating the entrance canopy and the wishbone columns supporting it, plays a small but significant role in the movement toward the main event. Flanking either side of the wishbone structure and mounted in recesses beneath the pavers, two 75-watt tungsten halogen MR-16 flood lights accent the leading edge of the canopy. Specially gasketed for outdoor use, the MR-16s, chosen for their good color rendering capability and broad beams, illuminate both the wishbone structure and the underside of the canopy with a wash of white light. Its transformers are also remotely located beneath nearby pavers for easy maintenance.

Detail Two: Luminous Screen

The glowing planes characterizing the Center for the Arts' main entrance lobby are also present at the secondary entrance lobby facing Mission Street. Like the main lobby, this space is a glowing light box with high-color-rendering fluorescent lights washing its yellow wall. It is distinguished by a 30-by-30-foot perforated aluminum vertical screen cantilevered above its entrance and partially covering its balcony-level facade. Designed to serve as a gigantic projection screen featuring upcoming events or a billboard supporting banners and posters, the screen, when lighted at night, is also a luminous sculptural component in the amalgam of geometric forms comprising the theater.

Mounted to the building with steel brackets and cables and supported by a grid of steel pipes echoing the 6-foot building module, the screen is illuminated from above by five 175-watt standard metal halide fixtures on 3-foot-long custom brackets. The brackets are attached to ballasts bolted to the grid and aligned in a rhythm that also reinforces the module. At 4,000 degrees

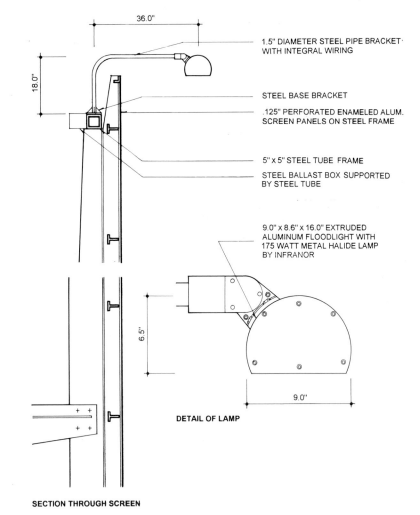

1.5" DIAMETER STEEL PIPE BRACKET WITH INTEGRAL WIRING

STEEL BASE BRACKET

.125" PERFORATED ENAMELED ALUM. SCREEN PANELS ON STEEL FRAME

5" x 5" STEEL TUBE FRAME
STEEL BALLAST BOX SUPPORTED BY STEEL TUBE

9.0" x 8.6" x 16.0" EXTRUDED ALUMINUM FLOODLIGHT WITH 175 WATT METAL HALIDE LAMP BY INFRANOR

DETAIL OF LAMP

SECTION THROUGH SCREEN

©1995 Polshek and Partners, LLP

Kelvin and with an effective color rendering index of 70, the metal halide sources enhance the silvery anodized aluminum surface of the screen and have a reasonable color rendering capability to illuminate the images that might be projected onto the screen.

Since evenly illuminating the surface of the screen was a primary objective, initial plans included uplight illumination from the base of the screen, but the architect wanted a clear view, unobstructed by light, through the perforated screen from the interior balcony. To achieve as uniform a wash of light as

possible on the screen, the position of the fixtures was calculated to avoid scalloped beam patterns. The reflectors produce overlapping narrow beam patterns that punch light toward the bottom of the screen. Power is supplied from the building to the fixtures by wiring threaded through the steel pipes. The 10,000-hour lamp life of the sources also keep maintenance concerns to a minimum.

The interplay of luminous planes—one soft and silvery the other warm and glowing—is enriched by the semi-transparency of the perforated screen.

Civic Arts Plaza

Location: Thousand Oaks, California

Architect: Antoine Predock

Architect of Record: Dworsky Associates

Lighting Designer: Lighting Design Alliance

Date Completed: August 1994

Photography: Timothy Hursley

Characteristically tied to the landscape, Antoine Predock's Civic Arts Plaza in Thousand Oaks, California, is a massive amalgam of austere volumes sheathed in wheat-colored stucco. His largest institutional project to date, the Civics Arts Plaza houses government offices, council chambers, and a 1,800-seat theater among other spaces. One of the Plaza's highlights is the theater's exterior wall into which are modeled an array of symbols related to its locale. The most enchanting in this abstract composition is a constellation of stars which infuses the stark wall with glistening points of light.

Each twinkling star in the galaxy is actually a Lucite rod which transmits

reflected light, like a gigantic fiber-optic cable, from the interior space behind the wall. Ranging in size from 1 to 4 inches in diameter to mimic the appearance of the brighter and fainter stars in the night sky, the Lucite rods embedded in the wall not only produce a shimmering Milky Way when viewed from the outside at night, but alternatively recreate the starry image on the interior wall of the theater's balcony vestibule when illuminated by the sunlight during the day.

Finely polished to work like prisms refracting either the reflected light from within or daylight from outside, the Lucite rods are surrounded by brass rings which form a waterproof juncture at the outside surface and cleanly finish the perimeters of the stars with a surface from which the stucco can be screeded. While the smaller Lucite rods are flush with the exterior surface, the larger ones extend four inches beyond the wall as sculptural relief. Inside, all of the rods are flush with the interior wall surface, painted a violet-blue to echo the twilight sky and keep the light level low in the vestibule, which is a light-locked zone directly adjacent to the theater hall. Nevertheless the walls reflect enough light from the vestibule's six ceiling-recessed 150-watt PAR 30 flood lamps and its handful of entrance downlights to illuminate the entire galaxy, which spans 19 feet in height and 65 feet in length.

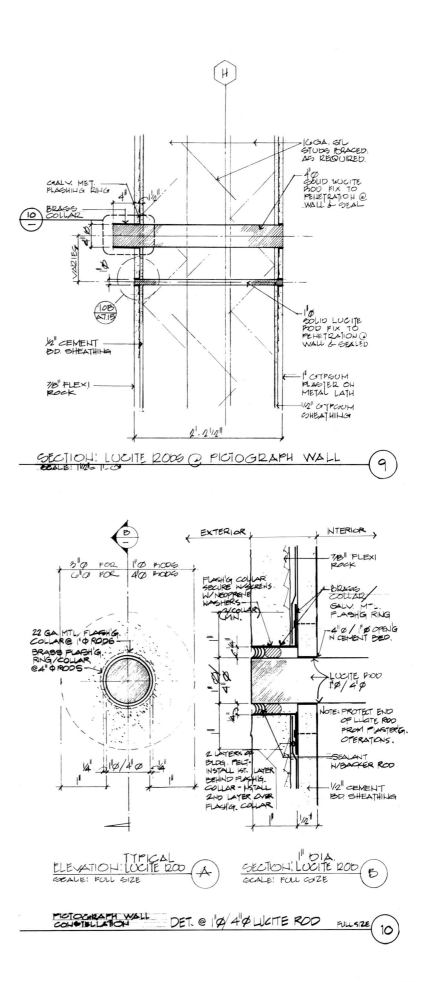

THE NELSON FINE ARTS CENTER, ARIZONA STATE UNIVERSITY

Location: Tempe, Arizona

Architect: Antoine Predock Architect

Lighting Designer: Antoine Predock

Manufacturer: Prescolite (70-watt high pressure sodium lamps)

Date Completed: April 1989

Photography: Timothy Hursley

As difficult as it may be to imagine a successful synthesis of pop culture and a reverence for nature, such an unlikely combination exists in architect Antoine Predock's design for the Nelson Fine Arts Center at Arizona State University. The most exquisite union of these contrary notions appears in the art center's exteri-

or plaza, where Predock gracefully melds architectural metaphors for desert history and drive-in movies. The plaza, a multi-purpose performance space consisting of layers of broad terraces juxtaposed against a medley of cool concrete buildings (including a fly tower which is transformed into an outdoor movie screen at night), is the heart of the plan. Literally and figuratively a stage set, the plaza is also where the architect's intent to engage a range of the senses most fully comes to life. Here, the gentle sound of flowing water in fountains complements the soft scents of herbs planted in shallow bowls and the smooth texture of stuccoed concrete surfaces.

Periodic points of light, an earthly extension of the starry canopy of the night sky above, figure prominently as a visual component of the sensory experience.

While all of the exterior lighting was deliberately designed to be downplayed—most of it indirectly reflecting off buildings surfaces to set a quiet, candlelit mood—one particular constellation of lighting elements subtly calls apt

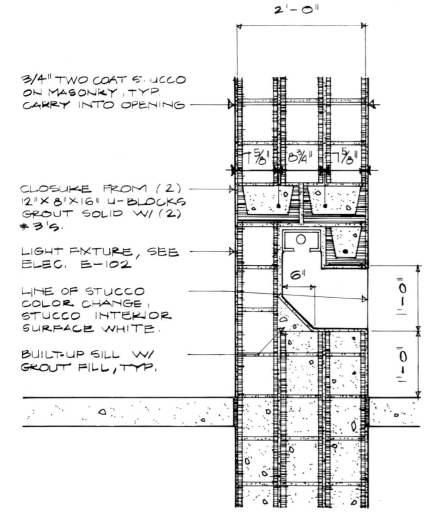

attention to one of the most visually compelling architectural elements surrounding the plaza area: a "mountain" of bleachers defining the plaza's northern boundary. A peaked wall along each side of the bleachers is outlined by a series of lighting recesses, which, along with several other lighting compositions in the surrounding buildings, softly punctuate the earthy backdrop of architectural forms.

The bleachers face both an outdoor performance platform beyond a brick arcade that curves in front of the dance studio building with the fly tower rising behind it. The recessed lighting that punctuates the inner surfaces of the bleachers' walls was designed not so much to illuminate the stepped treads as to define them. Positioned at every fourth tread, the 70-watt, high-pressure sodium sources provide enough rhythmic illumination to guide visitors up and down the steps, yet their relatively low-wattage and indirectness limit their brightness so as not to interfere with the viewing of nighttime performances or outdoor movies. The indirect sources were also positioned within a foot of the walking surfaces, below the eye level of visitors seated on the bleachers, to further limit glare.

The 2-foot-thick, stucco-coated, concrete-block wall was built to accommodate 1-foot-square apertures into which the high-pressure sodium lamps are recessed. The clear-lensed lamps are surface-mounted to junction boxes inside the aperture and pointed downward to reflect the light outward. The stucco is carried inside the aperture. The warm light of the high-pressure sodium sources contrasts with the cooler concrete surfaces, eliciting the candlelit effect. All exterior lighting is connected to an automatic timer.

PROMENADE

Location: Atlanta, Georgia

Architect: Thompson, Ventulett, Stainback & Associates

Lighting Designer: David A. Mintz, Inc., Lighting Consultants

Manufacturers: Sylvania (MR-16s); Bergen Art Metal (fabricator).

Date Completed: October 1990

Photography: David A. Mintz

With increasing competition among developers to have their buildings stand out in the nighttime sky, more attention is paid than ever before to illuminating exterior facades. In designing Atlanta's 38-story Promenade tower, architects Thompson, Ventulett, Stainback & Associates worked with lighting designers David A. Mintz, Inc., Lighting Consultants to create a distinctive nighttime identity for the structure that is as cultivated at its top as it is at its base. Equally important to the developers was encouraging pedestrian activity at the street level, which is decidedly lacking in the midtown area where the building is located. In response to both demands, the lighting designers created an array of custom lighting features that are thematically linked to the building's structure.

The genesis for all of the fixtures, inside and out, started with the lighting treatment of the building's top, which is characterized by metal epaulets positioned on each of its quirk corners and illuminated by metal halide spots. One of the more clever variations on that theme is a series of decorative sconces that were designed to integrate with the building's granite-faced concrete promenade at street level and link thematically with the top.

The sconce was designed to provide a shimmering crystalline light. Positioned at a height of 8 feet above the ground and mounted to a series of twin columns along the building's facade, the sconces are composed of a two-part 30-inch-high chrome-plated steel frame containing an MR-16 source hidden at its base. A custom-designed, square-shaped light pipe above the lamp and

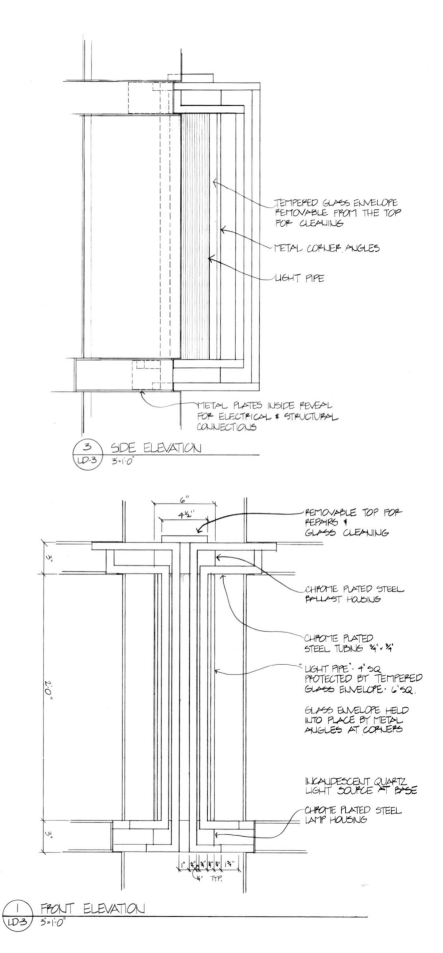

TEMPERED GLASS ENVELOPE REMOVABLE FROM THE TOP FOR CLEANING

METAL CORNER ANGLES

LIGHT PIPE

METAL PLATES INSIDE REVEAL FOR ELECTRICAL & STRUCTURAL CONNECTIONS

③ SIDE ELEVATION
LD-3   3=1'-0"

REMOVABLE TOP FOR REPAIRS & GLASS CLEANING

CHROME PLATED STEEL BALLAST HOUSING

CHROME PLATED STEEL TUBING ¾" × ¾"

LIGHT PIPE: 4" SQ PROTECTED BY TEMPERED GLASS ENVELOPE: 6" SQ.

GLASS ENVELOPE HELD INTO PLACE BY METAL ANGLES AT CORNERS

INCANDESCENT QUARTZ LIGHT SOURCE AT BASE

CHROME PLATED STEEL LAMP HOUSING

① FRONT ELEVATION
LD3   3=1'-0"

supported by the frame allows the crystalline quality of light to be achieved while the source remains invisible. A polished metal reflector at the top of the sconce reflects the light of the MR-16 back along the light pipe, whose prismatic film evenly refracts the light.

Its outdoor location prompted the development of some of the sconce's finer points. Because the light tube is not an outdoor material, for instance, it was enclosed with glass. With the natural expansion and contraction that occurs as the temperature warms up or cools down, however, it isn't possible to have a completely sealed fixture, which means that air and dirt eventually make their way inside. To avoid excessive maintenance, the designers equipped the sconce with a custom charcoal filter at its base.

Finally, the sconce's frame was developed to accommodate the dimensional variations in the reveals in the columns to which it is mounted. One part of the frame was designed to slip into the other, and the assembly was then telescoped into place and secured by set screws to metal mounting plates when the adjustments were complete.

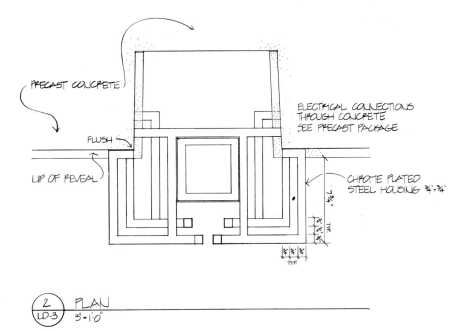

SCRIPPS CROSSING PEDESTRIAN BRIDGE

Location: San Diego, California

Bridge Design: Frieder Seible Engineer

Design Consultants: Safdie Rabines Architects, Adele Naude Santos & Associates

Lighting Design: Safdie Rabines Architects

Electrical Engineers: Engineering Dynamics (formerly DLSK Professional Engineers)

Structural Engineers: SEQAD Engineers, Burkett & Wong Engineers

Manufacturer: Bench light: Fiberstars (fiber optic cable, metal halide lamps).

Date Completed: October 1993

Photography: Becky Cohen and Frieder Seible

Detail One: Bridge Light

The Scripps Crossing Pedestrian Bridge, which traverses San Diego's scenic La Jolla Shore Drive, is a key link between the upper campus of the University of California and the research pier of the Scripps Institute of Oceanography. Developed by Frieder Seible Engineer with Safdie Rabines Architects, who were brought on at the schematic stage and served as design consultants through completion, the 140-foot-long, wheelchair-accessible bridge is an elegant structure composed of a cast concrete walkway suspended from a single eccentric concrete pylon and anchored by cables encased in stainless-steel tubes. In order to make the bridge useable night and day, the architects incorporated a recessed lighting feature which heightens its exquisite structure in the evening and fulfills functional illumination requirements for circulation.

The challenge was to illuminate the walkway for good visibility and security with a source that would be energy-efficient, easy to maintain, and virtually vandal-proof. At the same time the architects wanted to accentuate the slender cross section of the bridge without interfering with the transparency and lightness of its cabled support system or obstructing the views beyond. The solution was to use recessed downlighting below the base of the bridge's ribbed handrail.

Mounted to the edge of the concrete slab on both sides of the bridge are 1/4-inch-thick steel plates, which serve as the base of the handrail and conceal linear fluorescent downlights running along the length of the bridge. Surface mounted to the steel plates only 4 inches above the concrete, the fluorescent sources provide a concentrated wash of light on the walkway, reflecting off its concrete surface to illuminate the handrail and the cables. The reflected light is strong enough to fully illuminate the entire length of the cables, which rise 40 feet above the bridge. The 4-foot-long T-12 fluorescents with integral ballasts were designed to fit end to end between each of the slender vertical supports of the handrail. Their placement creates a punctuated rhythm of continuous light along the gentle curve of the bridge from beginning to end, while the unlighted supporting structure below the bridge disappears into darkness.

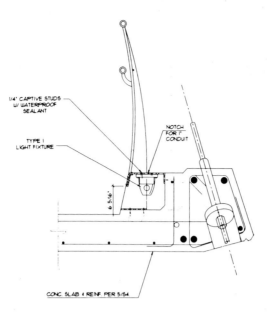

1/4" CAPTIVE STUDS
W/ WATERPROOF
SEALANT

NOTCH
FOR 1"
CONDUIT

TYPE 1
LIGHT FIXTURE

6 5/16"

CONC. SLAB & REINF. PER 5/S4.

Scripps Crossing Pedestrian Bridge

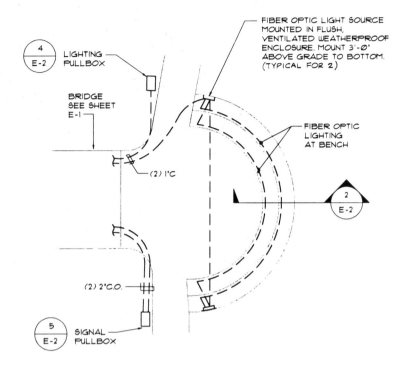

(4/E-2) LIGHTING PULLBOX

BRIDGE SEE SHEET E-1

FIBER OPTIC LIGHT SOURCE MOUNTED IN FLUSH, VENTILATED WEATHERPROOF ENCLOSURE. MOUNT 3'-0' ABOVE GRADE TO BOTTOM. (TYPICAL FOR 2)

FIBER OPTIC LIGHTING AT BENCH

(2) 1"C

(2) 2'C.O.

(2/E-2)

(5/E-2) SIGNAL PULLBOX

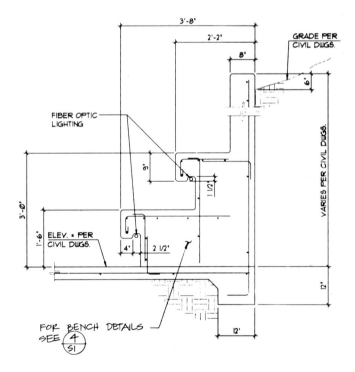

3'-8'

2'-2'

8'

GRADE PER CIVIL DWGS.

6'

FIBER OPTIC LIGHTING

VARIES PER CIVIL DWGS.

9'

1 1/2'

3'-0'

1'-6'

ELEV. = PER CIVIL DWGS.

4'

2 1/2'

12'

12'

FOR BENCH DETAILS SEE (4/S1)

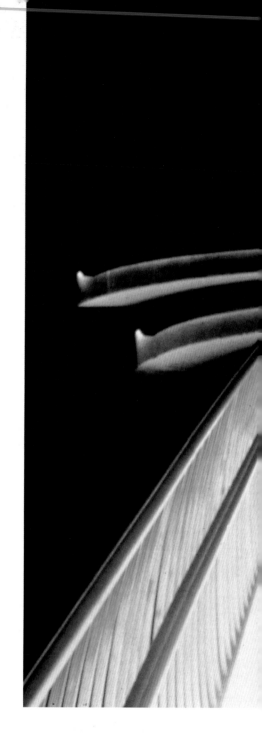

Detail Two: Seating Light

The bridge is anchored between a gently sloping hill on one side and a 3-story elevator tower overlooking the ocean on the other. To reinforce the sense of beginning and end, architects created a false perspective in the walkway by narrowing it in width from the hill to the tower side, dramatizing the view of the ocean horizon beyond the bridge's edge.

Additional views of the ocean can be seen from a semi-circular concrete seating area, which culminates the crossing on the hill side of the bridge. Like the gentle curves of the bridge, the semi-circular form of the bench is also highlight-ed with recessed lighting. The 25-foot-diameter concrete bench is composed of two concentric seating platforms, one above the other, embedded in the hill-side. Illuminating the interior curves of each platform are two single strands of 1/2-inch-diameter Britepak fiber-optic cable. These are mounted with a clear silicone adhesive in narrow, recessed grooves running lengthwise below the seats. Two 150-watt metal halide lamps, concealed in lamp compartments on either side of the bench, illuminate both cables from opposite ends. The lamp was chosen for its near-white color and long lamp life of 6,000 hours.

Index